The **ABC** Travel
Greenbook

Created by Martinique Lewis

INTRODUCTION

The late, great Maya Angelou once said, "You can't know where you're going, if you don't know where you've been." With the state of the world today, those words have never rang truer. As an avid Black traveler seeking out those who look like me from country to country has always been a top priority. It wasn't until I started the research for this book that I realized people of the African diaspora are EVERYWHERE!

Because our history has been hidden and sometimes erased, it's important for a resource like this to exist. The Greenbook holds the information that even Google can't tell you. In it are the communities, restaurants, festivals, and more that have been overlooked by travel publications. This resource honors our roots, celebrates Black owned businesses, and helps keep the Black dollar strong globally so that we can preserve them for generations to come.

Victor Hugo Green laid the foundation from the 1930s to1960s with the Negro Motorist Greenbook, with the aim of keeping African Americans safe on their journeys up and down US Route 66. Taking a page from his book, I want to keep Black travelers safe and connected on their journeys no matter where they're headed throughout the globe.

This book is for Black travelers of every age, every creed, and every origin. It's for the expat looking to connect with Black communities in their new home. It's for the boomer wanting to take a Black history tour in Amsterdam. It's for the millennial who wants to know what Black festivals are happening in Australia over the summer. And it's also for the Black athlete who wants to connect with the Black ski club in London. This is for us, by us, on every continent, in every country. This is the ABC Travel Greenbook the #1 resource connecting the african diaspora globally!

When you are traveling to any place in this book, please mention the ABC Travel greenbook, and let them know found them.If they haven't heard about this resource, please tell them to contact us at info@abctravelgreenbook.com

DEDICATION

This book is dedicated to all those who have helped shape and mold me along this journey. There are too many to mention but know that I am eternally grateful.

To Ruby Lewis, my 102 year old Abuela! A Panamanian immigrant who until this day inspires me to be my best creative self. As the Matriarch of our family her Panamanian roots have always made us proud to be connected to that country. An avid traveler herself , I know I make her proud as I strive to make this world a better place, just like her.

To Cynthia Black. My amazing mother, cheerleader, lightholder and SHERO! Who has always celebrated my uniqueness. The one that constantly tells me I can, I will, and one day people everywhere will be clapping for me. The one whose fostered my love for travel by taking me on domestic and international trips my entire life. From dropping me off to school in London, accompanying me at trade shows in Tokyo or chasing waterfalls with me in Costa Rica, I couldn't ask for a better mother. It is always my goal to make you proud.

To my intelligent, beautiful, bossy and dramatic niece, Cheyenne Marie Jackson! I don't have children yet, so everything I do, is for you. You are one of my best friends, and I work hard, to make sure you don't have to deal with racism when you travel the world in the future. Continue to learn, continue to ask questions and continue to be you. Thank you for the joy you bring.

And last, but certainly not least. To Victor Huge Green. A true hero, pioneer and leader in the travel space. For you to have created such a resource like the Negro Motorist Greenbook during a time when we were unwanted, is beyond incredible. You dedicated your life, to saving ours every time we traveled. Your work continues to inspire us all. We are forever grateful for the mark you left on this world, and it is my commitment to teach the world about you. Because of you I can, thank you.

CARD OF APPRECIATION

As the creator of this guide I wish to publicly thank all the communities in the Black Travel Movement and Black entrepreneurs who have partnered with me to bring this travel resource before travelers globally. Thank you for all your suggestions and knowledge contributed to keep the ABC Travel Greenbook up to date, so that we as a community have something authentic made for us by us, and to our preferences.

I hope that if you're using the ABC Travel Greenbook you will share it with all those who have an interest in connecting with the African Diaspora globally.

I have given you a selection of listing that you might choose from and include in your itineraries. Under no circumstances do these listing imply that the business is recommended.

EXPLANATION

I have worked tirelessly to make this guide as near complete as possible with extensive research and recommendations from locals across the world. Please note that this resource will constantly change with the opening and closing of black owned businesses.

Due to Covid19 we are asking for your cooperation with businesses being open to the public at limited capacities, strictly online, or not at all. With travel being more domestic due to the pandemic, this guide is still resourceful no matter your location. It is our hope that this resource is the reason businesses stay open, and we support each other through patronage and promotion. We welcome all feedback and suggestions that will improve this resource.

Contents

ABC Travel Greenbook Quick Guide

Want to find Black Travel information quickly? This portion of the book was put into place to give you the solutions you need! It also offers resources to black travelers and travel professionals to locate things of interest that don't necessarily have a home according to continent, country or city.We know we can find a large amount of information on America with ease, but we put it together in one place here. If there was something overlooked please email us at info@abctravelnetwork.com so It can be added.

Accommodations

Africa

African Bush Camps - 3 locations

Botswana

Linyanti Bush Camp
Linyanti Ebony
Linyanti Expeditions
Khwai Leadwood
Khwai Bush Camp
Migration Expeditions

Curiocity - 3 locations

Capetown

153 Main Rd, Green Point,
Cape Town, 8005, South Africa

Durban

55 Monty Naicker Rd, South Beach,
 Durban, 4001, South Africa

Johannesburg
302 Fox St, Jeppestown,
Johannesburg,
2094, South Africa

Capetown

iKhaya Lodge
4-5 Dunkley Square,
Cape Town, WC, 8001, South Africa

Ghana

Olma Colonial Suites
 Dadebu Rd, Accra, Ghana

Zaina Lodge
1 Yagbon Loop,
Mole National Park, Ghana

Liberia

RLJ Kendeja Resort & Villas
Roberts Field Highway –
Kendeja Village, RLJ Boulevard
Monrovia, Liberia

Morocco

Jnane Tamsna
Douar Abiad La Palmeraie
Marrakech, Morocco

Senegal

Sekubi
http://sekubi.com/
33 rue Bérenger Ferraud Dakar,
Sénégal

Soweto

Soweto Hotel & Conference
Center
Cnr Union Avenue & Main Road
Walter Sisulu Square of
Dedication
Kliptown, Soweto, Africa
South Africa

2Ten Hotel
Vhembe District, Limpopo
Province,
South Africa

AM Lodge
R40, Klaserie, Hoedspruit,
1391, South Africa

Euphoria Golf and lifestyle
R101, Mookgophong,
 0560, South Africa

Uganda

Primate Lodge Uganda
Susie House, 1st Floor, Ggaba
Road,
P.O.Box 33024

Kampala, Uganda

Zambia

Thorntree River Lodge

Zimbabwe

Bumi Hills Safari Lodge
Somalisa Campa
Somalisa Acacia
Somalisa Acacia
Somalisa Expeditions
Kanga Camp
Zambezi Expeditions
Nyamatusi Camps
Nyamatusi Mahogany
Khayelitshe House
Australia
The Village: Ikhaya lembali -
Glamping grounds
Wollongong, NSW, Australia
2529,
+61 420 449 769,
ikhayalembali@gmail.com

Carribean/ Centrsl& south American

Anguilla

Anguilla Great House Beach
Resort
http://www.anguillagreathouse.c
om/

Frangipani Beach Resort
Al2640 West End Village
Meads Bay, Anguilla

Paradise Cove Resort - Anguilla
P.O. Box 135,
Paradise Drive
The Cove, Anguilla
British West Indies

Bahamas

Hotel CTI
Meridian Highway
Rock Sound, South Eleuthera
Eleuthera & Harbour Island ,
Bahamas

Ocean West Boutique Hotel
West Bay Street
Nassau, Bahamas

Unique Hotels and Villas
North Palmetto Point
PO Box EL-25187
Governor's Harbour
Eleuthera, Bahamas

Belize

Black Orchid Resort
2 Dawson Lane, Burrell Boom
Village, Burrell Boom, Belize

Brazil

Red River Hostel
R. Marquês de Monte Santo,
290 - Rio Vermelho,
 Salvador - BA, 41940-330,
Brazil

Chez Cruza
A casa de

Cayman Islands

Westin Grand Cayman Seven
Mile Beach Resort & Spa
Seven Mile Beach P.O. Box
30620 Smb
Grand Cayman ,Cayman Islands

Colombia

Blue Apple Beach and
Townhouse
Isla Tierra Bomba, Blue Apple
Beach House,
Bocachica, Provincia de
Cartagena, Bolívar,
ColombiaIslabela
Isleta Cartagena, Colombia
 http://www.islabela.co/
+57 315 3972475

Dominican Republic

Ahnvee Resort & Sports
CALLE PEDRO CLISANTE N/S
EL BATEY, SOSUA, Dominican
Republic

Guadeloupe

La Creole Beach Hotel & Spa
Pointe de la Verdure, BP 61
97190
LE GOSIER ,Guadeloupe,
French West Indies
97190

3

Grenada

Spice Island Beach Resort
P.O. Box #6 Grand Anse Beach,
City Location: St. George's
State: Grenada, W.I.

Jamaica

Golden Castle Golf & Spa
The Greens, Lot 10
Rose Hall, Montego Bay.

The Runaway Jamaica
88 Rickets Drive
Runaway Bay, Jamaica

Villa Lolita Tryall
P.O. Box 1206
Montego bay, Jamaica

Half Moon, Jamaica
Rose Hall
Montego Bay St. James
JAMAICA WI

Negril Treehouse Resort
Norman Manley Blvd.
Negril, Jamaica

St.Croix

Carringtons Inn St. Croix
4001 Estate Hermon Hill
Christiansted
U.S Virgin Islands 00820

St.Kitts

Ocean Terrace Inn
P.O. Box 65, Wigley Avenue
Fortlands, St. Kitts

St. Kitts,West Indies

St.Lucia

Harbor Club St. Lucia, Curio
Collection by Hilton
Rodney Bay Marina
Gros Islet, Saint Lucia

Europe

Netherlands

Hostelle
Bijlmerplein 395
1102 DK Amsterdam

Ireland

Quayrest
9 Shannon Quays, Rooskey, Co.
Leitrim, N41 PY77, Irelan

United States

Alabama

Residence Inn Birmingham
Downtown at UAB
821 20th St.
Birmingham , AL 35205
Birmingham Marriott
3590 Grandview Parkway
Birmingham AL.

Arizona

Comfort Suites University of
Phoenix Stadium Area
9824 West Camelback Road
Glendale, Arizona 85305

4

The Glendale Gaslight Inn
5747 W. Glendale Ave
Glendale, Arizona 85301

Comfort Suites, Goodyear
15575 W. Roosevelt St.
Goodyear, Arizona 85338

Comfort Suites, Prescott Valley
2601 N. Crownpointe Dr.
Prescott Valley, Arizona 86314

Homewood Suites Phoenix Metro Center
2536 West Beryl Avenue
Phoenix, AZ 85021

California

DoubleTree by Hilton Hotel Berkeley Marina
200 Marina Blvd
Berkeley, CA 94710

HYATT House Cypress/Anaheim
5905 Corporate Ave.
Cypress, CA 90630

Embassy Suites Los Angeles-Downey
8425 Firestone Blvd.
Downey, CA 90241

Hilton Garden Inn San Francisco/Oakland Bay Bridge
1800 Powell Street
Emeryville, CA 94608

HYATT House Emeryville/San Francisco Bay Area

5800 Shellmound Street
Emeryville, CA 94608

Hyatt Place Fremont/Silicon Valley
3101 West Warren Avenue
Fremont, CA 94538

Hilton Garden Inn Los Angeles / Hollywood
2005 N Highland Avenue
Hollywood, CA 90068

Embassy Suites Irvine Orange County Airport
2120 Main Street
Irvine, CA 92614

Residence Inn Palo Alto Los Altos
4460 El Camino Real
Los Altos, CA 94022

Sheraton Gateway Los Angeles Hotel
6101 W. Century Blvd.
Los Angeles, CA 90045

Sonesta Hotel
1820 Barber Ln,
Milpitas, CA 95035

Pyramid Hotel Group
11950 Dublin Canyon Rd.
Pleasanton, CA 94588

HYATT house Santa Clara
3915 Rivermark Plaza
Santa Clara, CA 95054

HYATT house San
Diego/Sorrento Mesa
10044 Pacific Mesa Blvd.
San Diego, CA 92121

Courtyard San Francisco
761 Post Street
San Francisco , CA 94109

Sheraton Los Angeles San
Gabriel
 303 E. Valley Blvd.
San Gabriel, CA 91776

HYATT House San Jose/Silicon
Valley
75 Headquarters Drive
San Jose, CA 95134
HYATT house San Ramon
2323 San Ramon Valley Blvd.
San Ramon , CA 94583

Sheraton Fishermans Wharf
Hotel
 2500 Mason Street
San Francisco, CA 94133

Colorado

Denver Airport Marriott at
Gateway Park
16455 E. 40th Circle
Aurora CO 80011

Renaissance Boulder Flatiron
Hotel
500 Flatiron Boulevard
Broomfield, CO 80021

Colorado Springs Marriott
5580 Tech Center Drive

Colorado Springs , CO 80909
Hampton Inn & Suites Denver
Tech Center
5001 S. Ulster St
Denver , CO 80237

Fairfield Inn & Suites Denver
Cherry Creek
1680 South Colorado Blvd
Denver, CO 80222

Renaissance Denver Stapleton
Hotel
3801 Quebec St.
Denver, CO 80207

Residence Inn Denver
West/Golden
14600 W. 6th Avenue
Golden , CO 80401

 Courtyard Denver West/Golden
14700 W. 6th Ave.
Golden, CO 80401

Denver Marriott South at Park
Meadows
10345 Park Meadows Dr.
Littleton, CO 80124

Marriot Denver South at Park
Meadows
10345 Park meadows Dr.
Littleton, CO 80124

Courtyard Boulder Longmont
1410 Dry Creek Drive
Longmont, CO 80503

 Residence Inn Boulder
Longmont

1450 Dry Creek Drive
Longmont, CO 80503

SpringHill Suites Boulder
Longmont
1470 Dry Creek Drive
Longmont, CO 80503

Courtyard Boulder Louisville
948 West Dillon Road
Louisville, CO 80027

Residence Inn Boulder Louisville
845 Coal Creek Circle
Louisville, CO 80027

Springhill Suites Denver
North/Westminister
6845 W. 103rd Avenue
Westminster, CO 80021

Connecticut

Pyramid Hotel Group
18 Old Ridgebury Rd.
Danbury, CT 06810

Hartford/Windsor Marriott Airport
28 Day Hill Road
Windsor, CT 06095

Florida

AC Hotel Miami Aventura
20805 Biscayne Blvd.
Aventura , FL 33180

Aloft Miami Aventura
2910 Ne 207th St.
Aventura, FL 33180

Residence Inn Cape Canaveral
Cocoa Beach
8959 Astronaut Blvd
Cape Canaveral , FL 32920

Clearwater Beach Marriott Suites
on Sand Key
1201 Gulf Blvd.
Clearwater Beach, FL 33767

Hampton Inn & Suites
Clearwater / St. Petersburg -
Ulmerton Road
4050 Ulmerton Road
Clearwater, FL 33762

Hampton Inn & Suites Clermont
2200 East Highway 50
Clermont , FL 34711

The Henderson
200 HENDERSON RESORT
WAY
Destin , FL 32541

Embassy Suites Fort Myers-
Estero
10450 Corkscrew Commons
Drive
Estero, FL 33928

Hampton Inn & Suites Fort
Myers-Estero/FGCU
10611 Chevrolet Way
Estero, FL 33928

DoubleTree Grand Key Resort
3990 S. Roosevelt Blvd.
Key West , FL 33040

Fairfield Inn & Suites Key West

2400 North Roosevelt Blvd
Key West, Florida 33040

Reunion Resort
7593 Gathering Drive
Kissimmee , FL 34747

Aloft Miami Dadeland
7600 North Kendall Drive
Miami , FL 33156

Copper Door B&B
439, Northwest 4th Avenue,
Wynwood, Miami,
 Miami-Dade County, Florida,
33128
Hilton Cabana Miami Beach
6261 Collins Avenue
Miami Beach , FL 33140

The Gabriel Miami
1100 Biscayne Blvd
Miami , FL 33132

Fairfield Inn & Suites Naples
3808 White Lake Boulevard
Naples, FL 34117

SpringHill Suites Naples
3798 White Lake Blvd.
Naples, FL 34117

Fairfield Inn & Suites Orlando
Near Universal Orlando Resort
5614 Vineland Rd.
Orlando, FL 32819

Innisbrook Resort and Golf Club
36750 U.S. Highway 19 North
Palm Harbor, FL 34684

Hammock Beach Resort
200 Ocean Crest Drive
Palm Coast, FL 32137

Renaissance Fort Lauderdale-
Plantation Hotel
1230 South Pine Island Rd
Plantation, FL 33324

Hampton Inn & Suites Stuart-
North
1150 NW Federal Highway
Stuart , FL 34994

Embassy Suites Tampa
Downtown Convention Center
513 South Florida Ave.
Tampa, FL 33602

Hampton Inn Ft. Walton Beach
1112 Santa Rosa Boulevard
Walton Beach, FL 32548

Embassy Suites West Palm
Beach-Central
1601 Belvedere Rd. NE.
West Palm Beach, FL 33406

Hampton Inn West Palm Beach
Central Airport
1601 Worthington Rd
West Palm Beach, FL 33409

Hilton Garden Inn West Palm
Beach Airport
 1611 Worthington Rd
West Palm Beach, FL 33409

Georgia

Hilton Garden Inn Atlanta
North/Alpharetta
 4025 Windward Plaza
Alpharetta, GA 30005

Atlanta Marriott Perimeter Center
246 Perimeter Center Parkway
NE
Atlanta, GA 30346

Clarion Inn & Suites Atlanta
Downtown
186 Northside Dr SW
Atlanta, GA 30313
Courtyard Atlanta Buckhead
3332 Peachtree Rd NE
Atlanta , GA 30326

Hampton Inn Atlanta Perimeter
Center
769 Hammond Drive NE
Atlanta, GA 30328

Hyatt Centric Atlanta Midtown
125 10th Street NE
Atlanta, GA 30309

Residence Inn Atlanta
Midtown/Georgia Tech
1041 W Peachtree Street
Atlanta, GA 30309

 SpringHill Suites Atlanta Six
Flags
960 Bob Arnold Blvd.
Lithia Springs, GA 30122

Hawaii

Courtyard Waikiki Beach
400 Royal Hawaiian Avenue
Honolulu ,Hawaii 96815

Illinois

Fairfield Inn & Suites Chicago
Midway Airport
6630 South Cicero Avenue
Bedford Park, IL 60638

Sleep Inn Midway Airport
6650 S. Cicero Ave.
Bedford Park, IL 60638

Courtyard Chicago
Downtown/Magnificent Mile
165 East Ontario Street
Chicago, IL 60611

Holiday Inn Express & Suites
Chicago Midway Airport
6500 South Cicero Ave
Chicago, IL 60638

The Chicago South Loop Hotel
2600 S. State St.
Chicago, IL 60616
Chicago Marriott Suites Deerfield
2 Parkway North
Deerfield, IL 60015

Chicago Marriott Northwest
4800 Hoffman Blvd.
Hoffman Estates , IL 60192

Courtyard Chicago St. Charles
700 Courtyard Drive
St. Charles, IL 60174

Hampton Inn Chicago-Midway
Airport
6540 S. Cicero Ave.
Bedford Park, IL 60638

Amber Inn Hotel
3901 S. Michigan Avenue
Chicago, IL 60653

Courtyard Chicago Midway
Airport
6610 South Cicero Avenue
Chicago, IL 60638

Hilton Garden Inn
Chicago/Midway Airport
6530 S. Cicero Avenue
Bedford Park, IL 60638

Marriott Chicago Midway
6520 South Cicero Ave
Chicago, IL 60638

Residence Inn Chicago Oak
Brook
790 Jorie Boulevard
Oak Brook, IL 60523

Residence Inn Chicago
Naperville
28500 Bella Vista Parkway
Warrenville, IL 60555

Indiana

Hilton Garden Inn Bloomington
245 North College Avenue
Bloomington , IN 47403

Renaissance Indianapolis North
Hotel
11925 N. Meridian St.
Carmel , IN 46032

Courtyard Chicago Southeast /
Hammond
7730 Corinne Drive
Hammond, IN 46323

Fairfield Inn & Suites Chicago
Southeast / Hammond
7720 Corrine Drive
Hammond, IN 46323

Residence Inn Chicago
Southeast/Hammond
7740 Corinne Drive
Hammond, IN 46323

Courtyard Indianapolis at the
Capito
320 North Senate Avenue
Indianapolis, IN 46204

Hilton Indianapolis Hotel &
Suites
120 West Market St.
Indianapolis, IN 46204

Residence Inn Indianapolis
Downtown on the Canal
350 W New York Street
Indianapolis, IN 46202

Residence Inn Indianapolis
Fishers
9765 Crosspoint Boulevard
Indianapolis, IN 46256

Residence Inn Merrillville
8018 Delaware Place
Merrillville, IN 46410

Courtyard South Bend
Mishawaka

4825 N Main Street
Mishawaka, IN 46545

SpringHill Suites South Bend
Mishawaka
5225 Edison Lakes Parkway
Mishawaka, IN 46545

Kansas

Marriott Kansas City Overland
Park
10800 Metcalf Avenue
Overland Park, KS 66210

Kentucky

Cincinnati Airport Marriott
2395 Progress Drive
Hebron, KY 41048

Courtyard Louisville Northeast
10200 Champion Farms Dr
Louisville, KY 40241

Louisville Marriott Downtown
280 West Jefferson
Louisville, KY 40202

Residence Inn Louisville
Northeast
3500 Springhurst Commons
Louisville, KY 40241

Residence Inn Louisville
Downtown
333 East Market Street
Louisville, KY 40202

SpringHill Suites Louisville
Hurstbourne/North

10101 Forest Green Blvd
Louisville, KY 40223

Louisiana

Hilton Garden Inn New Orleans
Convention Center
1001 S. Peters St
New Orleans, LA 70130

Hotel Indigo
2203 St. Charles Ave.
New Orleans , LA 70130

Hubbard Mansion
3535 St. Charles Place
New Orleans, LA 70115

Maison dupuy
1001 Toulouse St.,
New Orleans, LA 70112

Nopsi
317 BARONNE ST.
NEW ORLEANS, LA 70112

The Moor
4511 Canal St., New Orleans ,
LA 70119

Maryland

TownePlace Suites Baltimore
Fort Meade
120 National Business Parkway
Annapolis Junction, MD 20701

The Ivy Hotel
205 E. Biddle Street
Baltimore, MD 21202

Phoenix Risin' Bed & Breakfast
1429 Bolton St.
Baltimore, MD 21217

Residence Inn Bethesda
Downtown
7335 Wisconsin Avenue.
Bethesda, MD 20814

TownePlace Suites Bowie Town
Center
3700 Town Center Boulevard
Bowie, MD 20716

DoubleTree Hotel Columbia
5485 Twin Knolls Rd
Columbia, MD 21045

Westin Baltimore Washington
Airport - BWI
1110 Old Elkridge Landing Road
Linthicum Heights , MD 21090

DoubleTree Hotel
Largo/Washington, DC
9100 Basil Court
Largo , MD 20774

Residence Inn National Harbor
Washington D.C
192 Waterfront Street
National Harbor , MD 20745

Residence Inn Silver Spring
12000 Plum Orchard Drive
Silver Spring, MD 20904

Sheraton Silver Spring Hotel
8777 Georgia Avenue
Silver Spring, MD 20910

Courtyard Waldorf
3145 Crain Highway
Waldorf , MD 20603

Hampton Inn Waldorf
3750 Crain Highway
Waldorf , MD 20603

Massachusetts

Marriott Residence Inn Boston
Harbor on Tudor Wharf
34-44 Charles River Ave.
Boston, MA 01129

Boston Marriott Burlington
1 Burlington Mall Road
Burlington , MA 01803

Hampton Inn & Suites Boston
Crosstown Center
811 Massachusetts Avenue
Boston, MA 02118

Shearer Cottage - Family Owned
& Operated
4 Morgan Avenue, Box 1063
Oak Bluffs, MA 02557

The Oak Buffs Inn
P. O. Box 2546
Oak Buffs, MA 02557

Embassy Suites
Boston/Waltham
550 Winter Street
Waltham, MA 02451

Residence Inn Boston Woburn
300 Presidential Way

Woburn, MA 01801

Michigan

Roberts Riverwalk Urban Resort
Hotel
1000 River Place Dr,
Detroit , MI 48207

Residence Inn Detroit Novi
27477 Cabaret Drive
Novi, MI 48377

New Mexico

Apache Canyon Ranch
#4 Canyon Drive
Laguna, NM 87026

New York

Akwaaba- 4 Locations

1.Mansion Brooklyn, NY
347 MacDonough St.
Brooklyn, NY 11233

2.115, Broadway, West Cape
May,
 Cape May County, New Jersey,
08204

3.3709, Baring Street,
Philadelphia,
Philadelphia County,
Pennsylvania, 19104

4.1708, 16th Street Northwest,
Dupont Circle, Washington D.C
., 20009

Urban Cowboy Brooklyn
111 Powers St.
Brooklyn , NY 11211

Quintessentials Bed & Breakfast
and Spa
8985 Main Road Box 574
East Marion, NY 11939

Hampton Inn Garden City
1 North Avenue
Garden City , NY 11530

Courtyard New York
Manhattan/Upper East Side
410 East 92nd Street
New York, NY 10128

Doubletree Metropolitan - New
York City
569 Lexington Avenue
New York, NY 10022

Fairfield Inn & Suites New York
Midtown Manhattan/Penn
Station
325 West 33rd St.
New York , NY 10001

North Carolina

Hampton Inn Raleigh/Cary
201 Ashville Avenue
Cary, NC 27518

Americas Best Value Inn
7900 Nations Ford Rd.
Charlotte, NC 28217

City Inn
7901 Nations Ford Rd.

Charlotte, NC 28217

Golden Green Hotel
3024 E. Independence Blvd.
Charlotte, NC 28205

Hampton Inn Charlotte-
University Place
8419 N. Tryon Street
Charlotte, NC 28262
HYATT house Charlotte/Center
City
435 East Trade Street
Charlotte, NC 28202

Le Méridien Charlotte
555 S. McDowell St. North
Tower
Charlotte, NC 28204

Ms. Elsie's Caribbean Bed &
Breakfast
334 N. Sharon Amity Rd.
Charlotte, NC 28211

Sheraton Charlotte Hotel
555 S. McDowell St. South
Tower
Charlotte, NC 28204

Hilton Garden Inn Raleigh-
Durham/Research Triangle Park
4620 South Miami Boulevard
Durham, NC 27703

Morehead Manor
914 Vickers Ave.
Durham, NC 27701

Four Points by Sheraton
Charlotte - Lake Norman

16508 Northcross Dr.
Huntersville, NC 28078

Fairfield Inn & Suites
Jacksonville
121 Circuit Lane
Jacksonville, NC 28546
TownePlace Suites Jacksonville
400 Northwest Drive
Jacksonville, NC 28546

Homewood Suites by Hilton
Raleigh-Crabtree Valley
5400 Homewood Banks Drive
Raleigh, NC 27612

Ohio

Henderson House B&B
1100 State Route 222
Bethel, OH 45106

Six Acres Bed & Breakfast
5350 Hamilton Ave
Cincinnati, OH 45224

Columbus Airport Marriott
1375 N. Cassady Ave.
Columbus, OH 43219

Embassy Suites by Hilton
Columbus
2700 Corporate Exchange
Columbus, OH 43231

Columbus Marriott Northwest
5605 Blazer Parkway
Dublin, OH 43017

Cincinnati Marriott Northeast
9664 S. Mason Montgomery Rd.

Mason, OH 45040

Cleveland Marriott East
26300 Harvard Rd.
Warrensville Heights, OH 44122

Cincinnati Marriott North
6189 Muhlhauser Drive
West Chester , OH 45069

Oregon

SpringHill Suites by Marriott
Portland Hillsboro
7351 NE Butler Road.
Hillsboro, OR 97214

Courtyard Portland City Center
550 SW Oak Street
Portland, OR 97204

Pennsylvania

Pittsburgh Marriott North
100 Cranberry Woods Dr.
Cranberry Township, PA 16066

Hilton Garden Inn Pittsburgh
University Place
3454 Forbes Avenue
Pittsburgh, PA 15213

Renaissance Pittsburgh Hotel
107 6th Street
Pittsburgh , PA 15222

SpringHill Suites Pittsburgh
Bakery Square
134 Bakery Square
Pittsburgh, PA 15206

DoubleTree Hotel Pittsburgh-
Meadow Lands
340 Racetrack Road
Washington, PA 15301

South Carolina

Clevedale
1050, Willis Road, Spartanburg
County,
South Carolina, 29301

Courtyard Charleston Historic
District Hotel
125 Calhoun Street
Charleston , SC 29401

Hotel Bennett
404 King St
Charleston, SC 29403

DoubleTree Resort by Hilton
Hotel Myrtle Beach Oceanfront
3200 South Ocean Boulevard
Myrtle Beach, SC 29577

Spartanburg Marriott
299 N. Church Street
Spartanburg, SC 29306

Tennessee

Hampton Inn Milan
15315 S. First Street
Milan, TN 38358

Hampton Inn & Suites Nashville-
Vanderbilt-Elliston Place
2330 Elliston Place
Nashville TN 37203

Hampton Inn
Nashville/Vanderbilt
1919 West End Avenue
Nashville, TN 37203

Urban Cowboy Nashville
1603 Woodland St
Nashville, TN 37206

Texas

Homewood Suites by Hilton
Dallas-Arlington
2401 Road to Six Flags Street
East
Arlington, TX 76011
Residence Inn Austin
Downtown/Convention Center
300 East 4th Street
Austin, TX 78701

SpringHill Suites Austin
North/Parmer Lane
12520 North IH.35
Austin, TX 78753

Courtyard Austin Airport
7809 E. Ben White Blvd
Austin, TX 78741

Courtyard Austin
Downtown/Convention Center
300 East 4th Street
Austin, TX 78701

Residence Inn Austin
North/Palmer Lane
12401 North Lamar Boulevard
Austin, TX 78753

Residence Inn Austin
Northwest/Arboretum
3713 Tudor Boulevard
Austin, TX 78759

Holiday Inn Austin NW Plaza /
Arboretum
8901 Business Park Drive
Austin, TX 78759

Fairfield Inn & Suites Austin
South
4525 South Interstate Hwy 35
Austin, TX 78744

Courtyard Austin South
4533 South IH.35
Austin, TX 78744

Austin Marriott South
4415 South IH.35
Austin, TX 78744

Courtyard Austin Northwest /
Arboretum
9409 Stonelake Boulevard
Austin , TX 78759

Hyatt House Austin/Arboretum
10001 N. Capital of Texas HW
Austin, TX 78759

SpringHill Suites Austin South
4501 South IH.35
Austin, TX 78744

Residence Inn Austin South
4537 South IH.35
Austin, TX 78744

Hyatt House Dallas/Uptown

2914 Harry Hines Boulevard
Dallas, TX 75201

Hyatt House Dallas/Lincoln Park
8221 N Central Expressway
Dallas, TX 75225

Hyatt Summerfield Suites
Dallas/Uptown
2914 Harry Hines Boulevard
Dallas, TX 75201

Sheraton Houston West Hotel
11191 Clay Road
Houston , TX 77041

Hilton Garden Inn Houston
Energy Corridor
12245 Katy Freeway
Houston, TX 77079

Residence Inn Houston
Downtown/Convention Center
904 Dallas Street
Houston, TX 77002

Houston Marriott Westchase
2900 Briarpark Dr.
Houston, TX 77042

Courtyard Houston by The
Galleria
2900 Sage Road
Houston, TX 77056
Residence Inn Houston by The
Galleria
2500 McCue Road
Houston, TX 77056

Hyatt House Houston/Galleria
3440 Sage Road

Houston, TX 77056

Courtyard Houston
Downtown/Convention Center
916 Dallas Street
Houston, TX 77002

SpringHill Suites Houston
Downtown/Convention Center
914 Dallas Street
Houston, TX 77002

Hampton Inn Houston I-10 East
10505 East Freeway
Houston, TX 77029

Wanderstay Houston
4018 Chartres St,
 Houston, TX 77004

Hampton Inn Houston-Near The
Galleria
4500 Post Oak Pkwy.
Houston, TX 77027

Courtyard Houston Brookhollow
2504 North Loop West
Houston, TX 77092

Homewood Suites Houston
Clear Lake
401 Bay Area Blvd.
Houston, TX 77058

La Maison in Midtown
 2800 Brazos
Houston, TX 77006

Courtyard Dallas DFW Airport
North/Irving
4949 Regent Blvd

Irving, TX 75063

DFW Airport Marriott South
4151 Centreport Drive
Fort Worth, TX 76155

Austin Marriott North
2600 La Frontera Blvd.
Round Rock, TX 78681

Hilton Garden Inn San Antonio
12828 San Pedro Avenue
San Antonio, TX 78216

Residence Inn San Antonio
Downtown/Market Square
628 S Santa Rosa Blvd
San Antonio, TX 78204

Fairfield Inn & Suites San
Antonio Downtown/Market
Square
620 South Santa Rosa
San Antonio, TX 78204

Courtyard Houston Sugar Land
12655 Southwest Freeway
Stafford, TX 77477

Residence Inn Houston Sugar
Land
12703 Southwest Freeway
Stafford, TX 77477

Hyatt Centric The Woodlands
9595 Six Pines, Suite 1100
The Woodlands, TX 77380

Wisconsin

Hyatt Place Madison/Downtown
333 West Washington Avenue
Madison , WI 53703

Virginia

Comfort Suites Suffolk-
Chesapeake
5409 Plummer Blvd
Suffolk, VA 23435

Salamander Resort & Spa
500 North Pendleton Street
Middleburg, VA 20117

Lady Neptune Inn at Shirley's
Beach House
507 North First St.
Hampton, VA 23664

 Magnolia House Inn
232 S. Armistead Ave.
Hampton, VA 23669

Washington DC

Residence Inn by Marriott
Washington
Downtown/Convention Center
 901 L Street, NW
Washington, D.C. 20001

Courtyard Washington, DC
Downtown/Convention Center
901 L Street, NW
Washington, D.C. 20001

Marriott Marquis Washington,
DC
 901 Massachusetts Avenue NW

Washingston , D.C 20001

Fairfield Inn & Suites
Washington DC/Downtown
 500 H Street NW.
Washington, D,C, 20001

Homewood Suites Washington,
D.C. Downtown
1475 Massachusetts, NW
Washington, D.C. 20005

Hyatt Place DC/Downtown/K
Street
1522 K Street, NW
Washington D.C. 20005

DoubleTree by Hilton Hotel
Largo/Washington DC
9100 Basil Court
Largo M.D 20774

Courtyard Washington,
DC/Dupont Circle
1900 Connecticut Avenue NW
Washington, DC 20009

Utah

Residence Inn Salt Lake City
(Airport)
4883 W Douglas Corrigan
Salt Lake City, UT 84116

Courtyard Salt Lake City
(Airport)
4843 W Douglas Corrigan
Salt Lake City, UT 84116

Airports with Black CEO's and Aviation directors

Baltimore-BWI- Ricky D. Smith

Birmingham-BHX-Ronald F. Mathieu

Long Beach- LGB-Cynthia Guidry

Montgomery-MGM-Marshall J. Taggart Jr.

Mobile-MOB-Chris Curry, C.M

New Orleans-MSY- Kevin Dolliole

Oakland-OAK- Bryant Francis

Richmond-Perry J. Miller-RIC

Santa Barbara -SBA- Henry Thompson

Seattle-Lance Lyttle

Toronto- YYZ- Deborah Flint

Banks

Alabama

1. One United Bank: Multiple ATM locations
2. Alamerica Bank: Birmingham
3. Citizens Trust Bank: Birmingham and Eutaw
4. Commonwealth National Bank: Mobile
5. Liberty Bank: Montgomery and Tuskegee
6. Metro Bank: Ashville, Heflin, Lincoln, Moody, Pell City, Ragland, Southside
7. Hope Credit Union: Montgomery

Alaska

1. One United Bank: Multiple ATM locations

Arizona

2. One United Bank: Multiple ATM locations

Arkansas

3. One United Bank: Multiple ATM locations
4. Hope Credit Union: College Station, Little Rock, Pine Bluff, and West Memphis

California

1. One United Bank: Multiple ATM locations, in addition to the Corporate Office and Crenshaw Branch, as well as the upcoming Compton Branch
2. Broadway Federal Bank: Los Angeles

Colorado

1. One United Bank: Multiple ATM locations

Connecticut

1. One United Bank: Multiple ATM locations

Delaware

1. One United Bank: Multiple ATM locations

District of Columbia

1. Industrial Bank: District of Columbia (Anacostia Gateway Banking Center, Ben's Chili Bowl, DC Court of Appeals, DC Superior Court, F Street Banking Center, Forestville Banking Center, Georgia Avenue Banking Center, J.H. Mitchell Banking Center, Nationals Park, Oxon

Hill Banking Center, U
Street Banking Center
2. Howard University
Employees Federal
Credit Union: C B Powell
Building

Florida

1. OneUnited Bank:
Multiple ATM locations,
in addition to the Miami
Branch
2. FAMU Federal Credit
Union: Tallahassee

Georgia

1. OneUnited Bank:
Multiple ATM locations
2. Carver State Bank:
Savannah
3. Citizens Trust Bank:
Atlanta, Decatur, East
Point, Lithonia, Stone
Mountain, Stonecrest
4. Unity National Bank:
Atlanta
5. 1st Choice Credit Union:
Atlanta
6. Credit Union of Atlanta:
Atlanta
7. Omega Psi Phi
Fraternity Federal Credit
Union: Toccoa

Hawaii

1. OneUnited Bank:
Multiple ATM locations

Idaho

1.OneUnited Bank: Multiple
ATM locations

Illinois

1. One United Bank:
Multiple ATM locations
2. GN Bank: Chicago
3. Liberty Bank: Forest
Park
4. South Side Community
Federal Credit Union:
Chicago

Indiana

1. One United Bank:
Multiple ATM locations

Iowa

1. One United Bank:
Multiple ATM locations
2. First Security Bank:
Aredale, Charles City,
Dumont, Hampton,
Ionia, Manly, Marble
Rock, Nora Springs,
Riceville, Rockford,
Rockwell, Rudd, and
Thornton

Kansas

1OneUnited Bank: Multiple
ATM locations
2.Liberty Bank: Kansas City

Kentucky

1. One United Bank: Multiple ATM locations
2. Liberty Bank: Louisville

Louisiana

1. One United Bank: Multiple ATM locations
2. Liberty Bank: Baton Rouge and New Orleans
3. Hope Credit Union: New Orleans
4. Southern Teachers & Parents Federal Credit Union: Baton Rouge and Thibodaux

Maine

1. One United Bank: Multiple ATM locations

Maryland

1. One United Bank: Multiple ATM locations
2. The Harbor Bank of Maryland: Baltimore, Randallstown, and Silver Spring

Massachusetts

1. One United Bank: Multiple ATM locations, in addition to the Corporate Headquarters and the Roxbury Branch

Michigan

1. One United Bank: Multiple ATM locations
2. First Independence Bank: Clinton Township and Detroit
3. Liberty Bank: Detroit

Minnesota

1. One United Bank: Multiple ATM locations
2. Mississippi
3. One United Bank: Multiple ATM locations
4. Liberty Bank: Jackson
5. Hope Credit Union: Biloxi, Drew, Greenville, Jackson, Louisville, Macon, Moorhead, Robinsonville, Shaw, Terry, Utica, and West Point
6. Missouri
7. One United Bank: Multiple ATM locations
8. Liberty Bank: Kansas City
9. St. Louis Community Credit Union: Ferguson, Florissant, Pagedale, Richmond Heights, St. John, St. Louis, University City, and Wellston
10. Montana
11. One United Bank: Multiple ATM locations
12. Nebraska

13. One United Bank: Multiple ATM locations
14. Nevada
15. One United Bank: Multiple ATM locations
16. New Hampshire
17. One United Bank: Multiple ATM locations
18. New Jersey
19. One United Bank: Multiple ATM locations
20. Industrial Bank: Newark
21. New Mexico
22. One United Bank: Multiple ATM locations
23. New York
24. One United Bank: Multiple ATM locations
25. Carver Federal Savings Bank: Brooklyn, Jamaica, and New York City
26. Industrial Bank: New York City
27. Urban Upbound Federal Credit Union: Long Island City

North Carolina

1. One United Bank: Multiple ATM locations
2. Mechanics & Farmers Bank: Charlotte, Durham, Greensboro, Raleigh, and Winston-Salem
3. First Legacy Community Credit Union: Charlotte
4. Greater Kinston Credit Union: Kinston

North Dakota

1. One United Bank: Multiple ATM locations

Ohio

2. One United Bank: Multiple ATM locations
3. Faith Community United Credit Union: Cleveland
4. Toledo Urban Federal Credit Union: Toledo

Oklahoma

1. One United Bank: Multiple ATM locations Oregon
2. One United Bank: Multiple ATM locations

Pennsylvania

1. One United Bank: Multiple ATM locations
2. United Bank of Philadelphia: Philadelphia
3. Hill District Federal Credit Union: Pittsburgh62

Rhode Island

1. One United Bank: Multiple ATM locations21

South Carolina

1. One United Bank: Multiple ATM locations
2. OPTUS Bank: Columbia
3. Brookland Federal Credit Union: West Columbia
4. Community Owned Federal Credit Union: Charleston

South Dakota

1. One United Bank: Multiple ATM locations

Tennessee

1. One United Bank: Multiple ATM locations
2. Citizens Bank: Memphis and Nashville
3. Tri-State Bank: Memphis
4. Hope Credit Union: Jackson and Memphis

Texas

1. One United Bank: Multiple ATM locations
2. Unity National Bank: Houston and Missouri City
3. Faith Cooperative Credit Union: Dallas
4. Mount Olive Baptist Church Federal Credit Union: Dallas
5. Oak Cliff Christian Federal Credit Union: Dallas

Utah

1. One United Bank: Multiple ATM locations

Vermont

1. One United Bank: Multiple ATM locations

Virginia

1. One United Bank: Multiple ATM locations
2. Virginia State University Federal Credit Union: South Chesterfield

Washington

1. One United Bank: Multiple ATM locations

West Virginia

1. One United Bank: Multiple ATM locations

Wisconsin

1. One United Bank: Multiple ATM locations
2. Columbia Savings & Loan: Milwaukee

Wyoming

1. One United Bank: Multiple ATM location

Black owned Bookstores

California

1 – Pyramid Art Books & Custom Framing
1001 Wright Avenue, Suite C
Little Rock, AR 72206
Owner/Proprietor:
Phone: 501-372-5824
Email:pyramidartbookscustomfra
ming@gmail.com
Opened in: 1988

2 – Nubian Nook
Court Street Hamilton
Bermuda, BM
Owner/Proprietor: Rosheena
Beek
Phone: 1 441-516-8258
Email: mommysays@yahoo.com
Opened in: 2017

3 – Ethnic Notions Bookstore
433 Solano Dr
Benicia, CA 94510
Owner/Proprietor:
Phone: 707-334-3060
Email:
Opened in: 2000
Last updated: 2014-03-21 (10)

4 – Smiley's Bookstore
940 East Dominguez Suite K
Carson, CA 90746
Owner/Proprietor:
Phone: (310) 324-8444
Email: info@SmileysBooks.org
Opened in: 1993

Last updated: 2014-04-04 (13)

5 – Hanna's Ethnic Bookseller
240 Blue Mountain Way
Claremont, CA 91711
Owner/Proprietor:
Phone: 909-626-5051
Email:
Opened in: 2000
Last updated: 2014-03-21 (11)

6 – Zahra's Books and Things
900 North La Brea Ave
Inglewood, CA 90302
Owner/Proprietor: Renee
Mendscole
Phone: 310-330-1300
Email:
Opened in: 2000

7 – Shades of Afrika Bookstore
1001 E 4th St.
Long Beach , CA 90802
Owner/Proprietor: Sista Renee
Quarles
Phone: (562) 436-2210
Email:
Opened in: 1994
Last updated: 2014-04-06 (140)

8 – Eso Won Bookstore
4327 Degnan Blvd.
Los Angeles, CA 90008
Owner/Proprietor: James Fugate
and Thomas Hamilton
Phone: (323) 290-1048
Email: jmfugate@msn.com
Opened in: 1990
Last updated: 2014-03-19 (4)

9 – Zambezi Bazaar
3347 W 43rd Street

Los Angeles, CA 90008
Owner/Proprietor: Jackie Ryan
Phone: (323) 299-6383
Email:
Opened in: 1990
Last updated: 2016-04-12 (135)

10 – Ashay by the Bay
1411 Webster Street
Oakland, CA 94612
Owner/Proprietor: Deborah Day
Phone: 1-844-543-7732
Email:
ashaybythebayceo@gmail.com
Opened in: 2017
Last updated: 2017-06-05 (175)

11 – Marcus Books (Oakland)
3900 Martin Luther King Jr. Way
Oakland, CA 94609
Owner/Proprietor: Johnson
Family
Phone: (510) 652-2344
Email:
info@marcusbooksoakland.com
Opened in: 1960
Last updated: 2017-06-05 (12)

12 – D3 Comic Book Spot
2148 Hilltop Mall Rd
Richmond, CA 94806
Owner/Proprietor: Darren Macon
Phone: 510-283-5051
Email:
d3comicbookspot@yahoo.com
Opened in: 2015
Last updated: 2020-06-04 (211)

13 – The Multicultural Children's
Book Store
1116 Hilltop Mall Drive

Richmond, CA 94806
Owner/Proprietor: Tamara
Phone: (510) 422-5304
Email:
multiculturalbookstore@gmail.co
m
Opened in: 2019
Last updated: 2020-02-04 (206)

14 – West County READS
Multicultural Children's Book
Store
2325 Hilltop Mall Drive
Richmond, CA 94806
Owner/Proprietor:
Phone: (510) 422-5304
Email:
Opened in: 2017
Last updated: 2018-04-25 (189)

15 – Carol's Books
1913 Del Paso Blvd
Sacramento, CA 95815
Owner/Proprietor: Carol
Phone: (916) 646-6525
Email:
Opened in: 2017
Last updated: 2017-06-04 (9)

16 – Underground Books
2814 35th Street
Sacramento, CA 95817
Owner/Proprietor: Georgia West
"Mother Rose"
Phone: 916-737-3333
Email: gwest@underground-
books.com
Opened in: 2002
Last updated: 2017-02-02 (110)

Connecticut

17 – Black Books Galore, Inc.
65 High Ridge Rd., #407
Stamford, CT 06905
Owner/Proprietor:
Phone:
Email:
Opened in: 1992
Last updated: 2014-08-19 (15)

District of Columbia

18 – DC Bookdiva's Mobile
Bookstore
Various Locations in DC
Washington, DC
Owner/Proprietor: T. Short
Phone:
Email: dcbookdiva@yahoo.com
Opened in: 0000
Last updated: 2014-03-19 (98)

19 – MahoganyBooks
1231 Good Hope Rd SE
Washington, DC 20020
Owner/Proprietor: Derrick and
Ramunda Young
Phone: 703-730-3873
Email:
customerservice@mahoganyboo
ks.com
Opened in: 2017
Last updated: 2017-11-23 (177)

20 – Sankofa Video Books &
Cafe
2714 Georgia Ave.,NW
Washington, DC 20001
Owner/Proprietor: Shirikiana
Gerima

Phone: 202-234-4755
Email: sankofa@gmail.com
Opened in: 1982
Last updated: 2012-03-24 (86)

21 – The Children Of The Sun
2802 Georgia Ave NW
Washington, DC 20001
Owner/Proprietor:
Phone: 202-299-0279
Email:
Opened in: 0000
Last updated: 2014-06-10 (147)

22 – Loyalty (Petworth)
Bookstore
843 Upshur NW
Washington, DC, DC 20910
Owner/Proprietor: Hannah Oliver
Depp
Phone: (240) 863-2087
Email:
hannah@loyaltybookstores.com
Opened in: 2019
Last updated: 2020-04-17 (208)

Delaware

23 – MeJah Books & Crafts
Holly Oak Plaza, 2099A
Philadelphia Pike
Claymont, DE 19703
Owner/Proprietor: Ms. Emlyn Q.
DeGannes
Phone: 302-793-3424
Email: mejahinc@yahoo.com
Opened in: 2000
Last updated: 2016-03-07 (16)

Dakar

24 – Chez Alpha Books
Behind YumYums-Ouakam
Cite Africa Dakar, Senegal, DKR
Owner/Proprietor: Angela
Franklin-Faye
Phone: +221 33 8206359
Email:
maizie@chezalphabks.com
Opened in: 2011
Last updated: 2019-11-09 (203)

Florida

25 – Pyramid Books
Boynton Beach, FL
Owner/Proprietor: Denise &
Shaka Akbar
Phone: 561-731-4422
Email: pyramidbks@aol.com
Opened in: 1993
Last updated: 2019-07-23 (91)

26 – Dare Books
245 N. U.S. Highway 17-92
Longwood, FL 32750
Owner/Proprietor: Desmond A.
Reid
Phone: 407-673-3273
Email:
DesmondR@darebooks.com
Opened in: 1982
Last updated: 2014-03-19 (118)

27 – The Gathering Awareness
and Book Center
314 N Devillers St
Pensacola, FL 32501
Owner/Proprietor: Georgia
Blackmon

Phone: (850) 438-4882
Email:
awarenessg@thegathering.gcco
xmail.com
Opened in: 1989
Last updated: 2017-12-03 (179)

28 – Cultured Books
833 22nd St. S.
St. Petersburg, FL 33712
Owner/Proprietor: Lorielle J.
Hollaway
Phone: (727) 328-4822
Email:
stpetereads@culturedbooks.com
Opened in: 2017
Last updated: 2017-12-18 (181)

29 – Best Richardson African
Diaspora Literature & Culture
Museum
1463 Tampa Park Plaza
Tampa, FL 33605
Owner/Proprietor: Skip
Richardson, Gigi Best-
Richardson
Phone: (813) 944-2112
Email:
bradlcmuseum@gmail.com
Opened in: 1997
Last updated: 2020-06-08 (193)

France

30 – Présence Africaine
25 bis rue des Ecoles 75005
Paris, FR 75005
Owner/Proprietor:
Phone: +33 (0)1 43 54 15 88
Email: presaf@club-internet.fr
Opened in: 1949

Last updated: 2019-07-27 (196)

Georgia

31 – Medu Bookstore,
Greenbriar Mall
2841 Greenbriar Parkway
Atlanta, GA 30331
Owner/Proprietor: Nia Damali
Phone: 404-346-3263
Email: nia@medubooks.com
Opened in: 1989
Last updated: 2014-03-19 (22)

32 – Sisters Bookshop
209 Edgewood Ave S.E.
Atlanta, GA 30303
Owner/Proprietor:
Phone: (404) 585-6243
Email: svbbooks@yahoo.com
Opened in: 0000
Last updated: 2014-04-04 (138)

33 – The Shrine of the Black
Madonna
946 Ralph D. Abernathy Blvd
SW
Atlanta, GA 30310
Owner/Proprietor:
Phone: 404-549-8676
Email:
buyer@shrinebookstore.com
Opened in: 1970
Last updated: 2019-11-06 (25)

34 – The Listening Tree
2308 Candler Rd.
Decatur, GA 30032
Owner/Proprietor: Omar and
Kimberly Finley
Phone:

Email:
listeningtreebooks@gmail.com
Opened in: 2014
Last updated: 2019-11-08 (204)

35 – Black Dot Cultural Center
6984 Main St.
Lithonia, GA 30058
Owner/Proprietor: Adigun
Kazemde Ajamu
Phone: 404-519-8107
Email: info@blackdotcc.com
Opened in: 2017
Last updated: 2018-12-13 (191)

36 – Book Boutique
2929 Turner Hill Rd
Lithonia, GA 30038
Owner/Proprietor: Rodney
Daniel and Monique S. Hall
Phone: 770-484-4595
Email:
bookboutiqueatl@gmail.com
Opened in: 2018
Last updated: 2018-12-10 (182)

37 – All Things Inspiration
Giftique
Mableton, GA
Owner/Proprietor: LaVonya
Tensley
Phone:
Email:
allthingsinspirationgift@gmail.co
m
Opened in: 0000
Last updated: 0000-00-00 (201)

38 – NuBian Books
1540 Southlak Pkwy, Ste 7A
Morrow, GA 30260

Owner/Proprietor: Marcus
Williams.
Phone: 678-422-6120
Email: marcus3x@yahoo.com
Opened in: 1999
Last updated: 2014-03-19 (24)

Illinois

39 – Lushena Bookstore
607 Country Club Drive, Unit E
Bensenville, IL 60106
Owner/Proprietor:
Phone: 630-238-8708
Email:
lushenabooks@gmail.com
Opened in: 0000
Last updated: 2012-03-24 (31)

40 – Da Book Joint
2311 E. 71 St
Chicago, IL
Owner/Proprietor: Verlean
Singletary
Phone: 773-655-3146
Email: verlean@dabookjoint.com
Opened in: 2007
Last updated: 2014-03-21 (124)

41 – Frontline Bookstore
5206 S Harper Ave
Chicago, IL 60615
Owner/Proprietor: Sekou
Phone: (773) 288-7718
Email:
Opened in: 1987
Last updated: 2014-03-14 (136)

42 – Semicolon Bookstore &
Gallery
515 N Halsted St

Chicago, IL 60642
Owner/Proprietor: DL Mullen
Phone: 312-877-5170
Email: info@semicolonchi.com
Opened in: 2019
Last updated: 2019-09-11 (199)

43 – The Underground
Bookstore
1727 E. 87th Street
Chicago, IL 60617
Owner/Proprietor:
Phone: 773-768-8869
Email:
TheUndergroundBookstore@gm
ail.com
Opened in: 1992
Last updated: 2014-03-19 (121)

44 – Black Expression Book
Source
9500 5 Western Ave
Evergreen Park, IL 60805
Owner/Proprietor:
Phone: 708-424-4338
Email:
Opened in: 2000
Last updated: 2014-03-19 (28)

45 – Afriware Books, Co
1701 S. 1st Ave., Suite 503
Maywood, IL 60153
Owner/Proprietor: Nzingha
Nommo
Phone: 708-223-8081
Email:
afriwarebooks@afriwarebooks.c
om
Opened in: 1993
Last updated: 2015-12-13 (27)

Indiana

46 – The Brain Lair Bookstore
714 E Jefferson Blvd
South Bend, IN 46617
Owner/Proprietor: Kathy M
Burnette, Book Dean
Phone: 574-400-5572
Email:
Opened in: 2018
Last updated: 2018-07-06 (190)

Jamaica

47 – Bookophilia
92 Hope Road
Kingston, JA
Owner/Proprietor: David Thomas
Phone: 1 876-978-5248
Email: info@bookophilia.com
Opened in: 2008
Last updated: 2016-03-27 (163)

Kentucky

48 – The Wild Fig Books
726 N. Limestone
Lexington, KY 40508
Owner/Proprietor: Ronald Davis
& Crystal Wilkinson
Phone: 859-381-8802
Email:
wildfigworkercooperative@gmail.
com
Opened in: 2011
Last updated: 2020-06-03 (89)

49 – Akoma Novelties & Books
1401 Triplett St. Suite. B
Owensboro, KY 42303
Owner/Proprietor: Brittney Odom
& Sharkoo Barrett

Phone: (812) 463-2427
Email:
info.akomalife@gmail.com
Opened in: 2015
Last updated: 2019-07-08 (192)

Louisiana

50 – SanKofa With Me
7720 Linwood
Caddo, LA 71106
Owner/Proprietor:
Phone: 318-560-1136
Email:
sankofawithme@gmail.com
Opened in: 2017
Last updated: 2017-12-26 (184)

51 – Word of Life Christian
Bookstores
6321 West Blvd.
Los Angeles, LA 90043
Owner/Proprietor: Jonathan
Curtiss
Phone: 323-295-8223
Email: jon@shopwordoflife.com
Opened in: 1961
Last updated: 2020-06-11 (214)

52 – Community Book Center
2523 Bayou Road
New Orleans, LA 70119
Owner/Proprietor: Vera Warren-
Williams
Phone: 504-948-7323
Email:
Opened in: 1983
Last updated: 2014-03-19 (34)

53 – <u>Nubian Cultural Outreach Center</u>
7720 Linwood Ave
Shreveport, LA 71106
Owner/Proprietor:
Phone: (318) 686-4477
Email:
Opened in: 0000
Last updated: 2014-04-06 (139)

London

54 – <u>New Beacon Books</u>
76 Stroud Green Road
United Kingdom, LN N4 3EN
Owner/Proprietor:
Phone: +44 20 7272 4889
Email: newbeaconbooksuk@gmail.com
Opened in: 1966
Last updated: 2019-07-27 (195)

Nigeria

55 – <u>The Jazzhole</u>
168 Awolowo Road
Ikoyi, LOS
Owner/Proprietor: Kunle Tejuosho
Phone: +234 706 064 8580
Email:
Opened in: 1991
Last updated: 2019-11-10 (205)

Massachusetts

56 – <u>Frugal Bookstore</u>
57 Warren Street Roxbury, MA 02119
Roxbury, MA 02119
Owner/Proprietor: Leonard Egerton

Phone: 617-541-1722
Email: frugal_books@yahoo.com
Opened in: 0000
Last updated: 2019-11-17 (119)

57 – <u>Olive Tree Books-n-Voices</u>
97 Hancock Street
Springfield, MA 01109
Owner/Proprietor: Zee Johnson
Phone: 413-737-6400
Email: olivetreebooks@msn.com
Opened in: 2004
Last updated: 2014-03-19 (42)

Maryland

58 – <u>MasterWorks Books</u>
2703 Curry Drive
Adelphi, MD 20783
Owner/Proprietor:
Phone: 301-422-2168
Email:
Opened in: 2000
Last updated: 2014-03-21 (36)

59 – <u>Everyone's Place</u>
1356 W. North Avenue
Baltimore, MD 21217
Owner/Proprietor:
Phone: 410-728-0877
Email:
Opened in: 1986
Last updated: 2014-03-19 (35)

60 – <u>Expressions Books and Frames</u>
222 N Paca Street
Baltimore, MD 21201
Owner/Proprietor:
Phone: (410) 783-0195
Email:

Opened in: 0000
Last updated: 0000-00-00 (166)

61 – Jay Books
400 W Lexington Street
Baltimore, MD 21201
Owner/Proprietor:
Phone:
Email:
Opened in: 0000
Last updated: 2016-05-13 (164)

62 – Vision Christian Bookstore
10398 Piscataway Road
Clinton, MD 20735
Owner/Proprietor: Robert &
Cheryl Woodard
Phone: 301-234-0035
Email: armorofgod@comcaat.net
Opened in: 2011
Last updated: 2017-12-21 (183)

63 – Wisdom Book Center
5116 Liberty Heights Ave.
Gwynn Oak, MD 21207
Owner/Proprietor: Bro. Tehuti &
Bro. Elliot
Phone: (410) 664-1946
Email:
wisdombookcenter@verizon.net
Opened in: 1997
Last updated: 2016-01-27 (162)

64 – Cartel Cafe & Books Store
5011 Indian Head Highway
Oxon Hill, MD 20745
Owner/Proprietor: T. Styles
Phone: 240 724-7225
Email:
cartelcafeandbooks@yahoo.com
Opened in: 2008

Last updated: 2014-03-19 (120)

65 – Loyalty Books
823 Ellsworth Drive
Silver Spring, MD 20910
Owner/Proprietor: Hannah Oliver
Depp
Phone: 443-466-6773
Email:
hannah@loyaltybookstores.com
Opened in: 2019
Last updated: 2020-04-17 (207)

66 – Silver Spring Books
938 Bonifant Street
Silver Spring, MD 20910
Owner/Proprietor: Cynthia
Parker
Phone: 301-587-7484
Email:
Opened in: 0000
Last updated: 2015-12-06 (159)

67 – Urban Knowledge
Bookstore
3731 Branch Avenue
Temple Hills, MD 20748
Owner/Proprietor:
Phone: (301) 702-0717
Email:
Opened in: 0000
Last updated: 2016-05-13 (165)

Michigan

68 – Source Booksellers
4240 Cass Ave Suite 105
Detroit, MI 48201
Owner/Proprietor: Janet Jones
Phone: 313-832-1155

Email:
info@sourcebooksdetroit.com
Opened in: 1989
Last updated: 2014-06-03 (146)

69 – Nandi's Knowledge Cafe
12511 Woodward Ave
Highland Park, MI 48203
Owner/Proprietor:
Phone: (313) 865-1288
Email:
Opened in: 0000
Last updated: 2014-11-08 (152)

70 – Detroit Book City
24361 Greenfield Rd, Ste. 305
Southfield, MI 48075
Owner/Proprietor:
Phone: (248) 209-6880
Email:
Opened in: 2016
Last updated: 2017-12-13 (180)

71 – The Truth Bookstore
21500 Northwestern Highway,
Northland Mall Store # 779
Southfield, MI 48075
Owner/Proprietor:
Phone: 248-557-4824
Email:
Opened in: 1994
Last updated: 2014-03-19 (92)

72 – Hood Book Headquarters
20900 Dequindre Road
Warren, MI 48091
Owner/Proprietor:
Phone:
Email:
Opened in: 2000
Last updated: 2014-03-21 (107)

73 – Black Stone Bookstore &
Cultural Center
214 W. Michigan Ave
Ypsilanti, MI 48197
Owner/Proprietor: Kip Johnson
and Carlos Franklin
Phone: (734) 961-7376
Email:
info.blackstoneproject@gmail.co
m
Opened in: 2013
Last updated: 2020-06-07 (134)

Minnesota

74 – Babycake's Book Stack

St. Paul, MN 55104
Owner/Proprietor: Zsamé
Morgan
Phone: 651-321-3436
Email:
zsame@babycakesbookstack.co
m
Opened in: 2019
Last updated: 2020-07-29 (221)

Missouri

75 – Willa's Books & Vinyl
1734 E 63rd Street
Kansas City, MO 64110
Owner/Proprietor: Willa
Robinson
Phone: (816) 419-1051
Email: willasbooks@gmail.com
Opened in: 1994

76 – Progressive Emporium &
Education Center

1108 North Sarah Ave.
St. Louis, MO 63113
Owner/Proprietor:
Phone: (314) 875-9277
Email:
progressiveemporium@yahoo.co
m
Opened in: 0000
Last updated: 2014-05-01 (144)

77 – EyeSeeMe
7827 Olive Blvd
University City, MO 63130
Owner/Proprietor: Pamela Blair
Phone: (314) 349-1122
Email:
customerservice@eyeseeme.co
m
Opened in: 2015
Last updated: 2016-01-15 (161)

Mississippi

78 – Magnolia Tree Books
310 N. Magnolia Street, Suite
101A
Laurel, MS 39440
Owner/Proprietor: zaji
Phone: 601-342-0990
Email:
info@magnoliatreebooks.com
Opened in: 2013
Last updated: 2014-03-21 (130)

Nebraska

79 – Aframerican Book Store
3226 Lake St
Omaha, NE 68111
Owner/Proprietor:

Phone:
Email: aframerican@yahoo.com
Opened in: 2000
Last updated: 2014-03-19 (44)

New Jersey

80 – The Little Boho Bookstore
164a Broadway
Bayonne, NJ 07002
Owner/Proprietor: Sandra Dear
& Rod Johnson
Phone: 2012584499
Email:
info@thelittlebohobookshop.com
Opened in: 2017
Last updated: 2020-06-20 (218)

81 – La Unique African American
Books & Cultural Center
111 N 6th St.
Camden, NJ 08102
Owner/Proprietor: Larry Miles
Phone: (856) 338-1958
Email:
Simba@launiquebooks.net
Opened in: 1992
Last updated: 2014-04-30 (143)

82 – African American Book
Store
216 1st St
Hackensack, NJ 07601
Owner/Proprietor:
Phone:
Email:
Opened in: 2000
Last updated: 2014-03-19 (45)

83 – Source of Knowledge
867 Broad St

Newark, NJ 07102
Owner/Proprietor: Dexter
George
Phone: (973) 824-2556
Email:
sourceofknowledge867@yahoo.
com
Opened in: 1998
Last updated: 2019-12-19 (157)

84 – Urban Books On Wheels
28 Old Tpke
Pleasantville, NJ 08232
Owner/Proprietor:
Phone: (609) 383-9100
Email: Futuredj1164@aol.com
Opened in: 0000
Last updated: 2014-03-21 (106)

85 – Imoya Treasures, Inc
1465 Irving Street
Rahway, NJ 07065
Owner/Proprietor:
Phone: 732-388-4955
Email:
Opened in: 2000
Last updated: 2014-03-21 (48)

Nevada

86 – Janco Books
2202 W Charleston Blvd
Las Vegas, Nevada 89102, NV
89102
Owner/Proprietor: Christina
Benton
Phone: 702-522-9286
Email:
books@jancobookstore.comOpe
ned
Opened in: 2017

Last updated: 2018-01-21 (185)

New York

87 – The Lit. Bar
131 Alexander Avenue (btwn
134th St. & Bruckner Blvd)
Bronx, NY 10454
Owner/Proprietor: Noëlle Santos
Phone: (347) 955-3610
Email:
thebronxreads@thelitbar.com
Opened in: 2019

88 – African Record Center
1194 Nostrand Ave
Brooklyn, NY 11225
Owner/Proprietor:
Phone: (718) 493-4500
Email:
Opened in: 2019
Last updated: 2020-06-16 (216)

89 – Black Mind Book Boutique
610 New York Ave
Brooklyn, NY 11203
Owner/Proprietor:
Phone: 718-774-5800
Email:
Opened in: 2000
Last updated: 2014-03-21 (52)

90 – Cafe con Libros
724 Prospect Place
Brooklyn, NY 11216
Owner/Proprietor: Kalima
DeSuze
Phone: 347-460-2838
Email:
info@cafeconlibrosbk.com
Opened in: 2017

Last updated: 2018-02-02 (186)

91 – Official Connection
312 Livingston Street
Brooklyn, NY 11217
Owner/Proprietor:
Phone: (718) 488-0006
Email:
official.connection@hotmail.com
Opened in: 2010
Last updated: 2015-08-13 (142)

92 – Zawadi Books
1382 Jefferson Avenue
Buffalo, NY 14208
Owner/Proprietor: Kenneth and
Sharon Holley
Phone: (716) 903-6740
Email: jordanholley@aol.com
Opened in: 2012
Last updated: 2017-12-12 (150)

93 – Grandma's Place
84 West 120th Street
Harlem, NY 10027
Owner/Proprietor: Grandma
Dawn
Phone: (212) 360-6776
Email:
grandmasplaceinc@email.biz
Opened in: 2009
Last updated: 2015-01-25 (154)

94 – Blenheim Hill Books
698 Main Street, Suite A
Hobart, NY 13788
Owner/Proprietor: Cheryl Clarke
Barbara Balliet &
Phone: 607-538-9222
Email:
blenheimbooks1@gmail.com

Opened in: 2005
Last updated: 2017-03-10 (172)

95 – Becoming Gods Answer
Bookstore
1832 Madison Ave (between
119th and 120th st)
New York, NY 10035
Owner/Proprietor: Rev Joyce
Eady
Phone: 646-215-6119
Email:
c.brown@becominggodsanswer
bookstore.com
Opened in: 0000
Last updated: 2014-03-19 (102)

96 – Sister's Uptown Bookstore
1942 Amsterdam Avenue (at
156th Street)
New York, NY 10032
Owner/Proprietor: Janifer P.
Wilson
Phone: 212-862-3680
Email:
Opened in: 2000
Last updated: 2014-03-19 (58)

97 – Mood Makers Books & Art
Gallery Village Gate Square
274 N. Goodman St.
Rochester, NY 14607
Owner/Proprietor:
Phone: 877.223.1730
Email:
sales@moodmakersbooks.com
or info@moodmakersbooks.
Opened in: 1994
Last updated: 2014-03-19 (56)

Ohio

98 – Smith & Hannon Book
Store
50 E Freedom Way
Cincinnati, OH 45202
Owner/Proprietor:
Phone: (513) 641-2700
Email:
info@smithandhannonbookstore.
com
Opened in: 2003
Last updated: 2019-09-11 (200)

99 – A Cultural Exchange
12624 Larchmere Blvd.
Cleveland, OH 44120
Owner/Proprietor: Deborah
McHamm
Phone: 216-229-8300
Email:
aculturalexchange@fsbcglobal.n
et
Opened in: 1991
Last updated: 2014-03-19 (64)

100 – The African Book Shelf
1324Q Euclid Ave
Cleveland, OH 44112
Owner/Proprietor:
Phone: 216-681-6511
Email:
Opened in: 2000
Last updated: 2014-03-21 (61)

101 – Black Art Plus
43 Parsons Ave.
Columbus, OH 43215
Owner/Proprietor: Mike Miller
Phone: 614-469-9980
Email: blackartplus@att.net

Opened in: 1987
Last updated: 2014-03-19 (62)

102 – The Book Suite
887 E. Long Street
Columbus, OH 43203
Owner/Proprietor: James
Phone: 614-252-4552
Email: james@thebooksuite.com
Opened in: 0000
Last updated: 2014-03-21 (112)

103 – Ujamaa Book Store
1493 E Livingston Ave
Columbus, OH 43205
Owner/Proprietor: Mustafaa
Shabazz
Phone: 614-258-4633
Email: juneteenthohio@fuse.net
or smustafaa@aol.com
Opened in: 1997
Last updated: 2014-03-19 (66)

Oklahoma

104 – Nappy Roots Books
3705 Springlake Drive
Oklahoma City, OK 73111
Owner/Proprietor: Camille
Landry
Phone: 405-896-0203
Email:
camille.landry@gmail.com
Opened in: 2018
Last updated: 2020-06-04 (212)

105 – Fulton Street Books &
Coffee
210 W Latimer Street
Tulsa, OK 74106

Owner/Proprietor: Onikah
Asamoa-Caesar
Phone: 918-932-8646
Email: info@fultonstreet918.com
Opened in: 0000
Last updated: 2020-06-09 (213)

106 – Mocha Books
5525 E 51ST STREET, SUITE
205
Tulsa, OK 74135
Owner/Proprietor: McGlory
Shionka
Phone: 918-236-9019
Email: mochabooks@gmail.com
Opened in: 2019
Last updated: 2019-11-03 (202)

Ontario

107 – Knowledge Bookstore
177 Queen Street West
Brampton, ON L6Y 1M5
Owner/Proprietor:
Phone: 905-459-9875
Email:
sales@knowledgebookstore.com
Opened in: 0000
Last updated: 2014-12-08 (153)

Pennsylvania

108 – The Black Reserve
Bookstore
319 W. Main Street, Suite #6
Lansdale, PA 19446
Owner/Proprietor: Anwar
Muhammad
Phone: 267-221-3090

Email:
theblackreservebookstore@gmai
l.com
Opened in: 2017
Last updated: 2018-03-24 (188)

109 – Books & Stuff
23 W Maplewood Mall
Philadelphia, PA 19144
Owner/Proprietor:
Phone:
Email: 215-844-0844
Opened in: 2015
Last updated: 2017-09-24 (176)

110 – Color Book Gallery
6353 Germantown Ave
Philadelphia, PA 19144
Owner/Proprietor: Deborah Gary
Phone: 215-844-4200
Email:
Opened in: 0000
Last updated: 2015-09-11 (156)

111 – Hakim's Bookstore and
Gift Shop
210 S 52nd St
Philadelphia, PA 19139
Owner/Proprietor:
Phone: (215) 474-9495
Email:
bookstorehakims@gmail.com
Opened in: 1959
Last updated: 2014-03-19 (70)

112 – Harriett's Bookshop
258 E. Girard Ave
Philadelphia, PA 19125
Owner/Proprietor: Jeannine
Cook
Phone:

Email:
info@harriettsbookshop.com
Opened in: 2020
Last updated: 2020-04-17 (209)

113 – Uncle Bobbie's Coffee &
Books
5445 Germantown Ave
Philadelphia, PA 19144
Owner/Proprietor: Marc Lamont
Hill
Phone: (215) 403-7058
Email:
Opened in: 2017
Last updated: 2017-11-27 (178)

114 – The Tiny Bookstore
1130 Perry Highway, Suite 106
Pittsburgh, PA 15237
Owner/Proprietor: Lea Bickerton
Phone: 412-585-2651
Email: info@tinybookspgh.com
Opened in: 2018
Last updated: 2020-06-15 (215)

South Carolina

115 – Turning Page Bookshop
216 Saint James Ave Ste F
Goose Creek, SC 29445
Owner/Proprietor: VaLinda Miller
Phone: 843-501-7223
Email:
Opened in: 2019
South Carolina

116 – Malcolm X Center for Self-
Determination
321 W. Antrim Drive
Greenville, SC 29606

Owner/Proprietor: Efia
Nwangaza
Phone: (864) 239-0470
Email: wmxp955@gmail.com
Opened in: 1991
Last updated: 2014-06-28 (149)

Tennessee

117 – The African Place
581 N 3rd St
Memphis, TN 38105
Owner/Proprietor:
Phone: (901) 524-0800
Email: theafricanplace@aol.com
Opened in: 0000
Last updated: 2015-11-02 (158)

118 – Alkebu-Lan Images
Bookstore & Gift Shop
2721 Jefferson Street
Nashville, TN 37208
Owner/Proprietor: Yusef Harris
Phone: 615-321-4111
Email:
alkebulanimages@gmail.com
Opened in: 1986
Last updated: 2015-01-07 (73)

Texas

119 – Pan-African Connection
828 Fourth Ave.
Dallas, TX 75226
Owner/Proprietor: Akwete
Tyehimba (CEO)
Phone: 214-943-8262
Email: panafric@airmail.net
Opened in: 1989
Last updated: 2014-03-19 (96)

120 – <u>Enda's Booktique</u>
428 N. Main Street
Duncanville, TX 75116
Owner/Proprietor: E Jean
Pemberton Jones
Phone: 972-460-6362
Email:
endasbooktique@gmail.com
Opened in: 2019
Last updated: 0000-00-00 (210)

121 – <u>The Dock Bookshop</u>
6637 Meadowbrook Dr.
Fort Worth, TX 76112
Owner/Proprietor: Donya
Craddock
Phone: 817-457-5700
Email:
thedockbookshop@gmail.com
Opened in: 2008
Last updated: 2014-03-19 (6)

122 – <u>African Imports Houston</u>
12300 North Fwy Ste 147
Greenspoint Mall
Houston, TX 77060
Owner/Proprietor: Obi
Phone: (281) 875-0056
Email: donbasel@yahoo.com
Opened in: 1997
Last updated: 2014-03-21 (131)

123 – <u>Black World Books</u>
500 N Fort Hood Street Suite
504
Killeen, TX 76541
Owner/Proprietor: Maeva
Jackson
Phone: (254) 554-5559
Email:
info@blackworldbooks.com

Opened in: 2016
Last updated: 2017-04-17 (173)

Virginia

124 – <u>Harambee Books and
Artworks</u>
1132 Prince Street
Alexandria, VA 22314
Owner/Proprietor:
Phone: 703-299-2591
Email: info@harambeebooks.org
Opened in: 2016
Last updated: 2018-02-05 (187)

125 – <u>Riches In Reading</u>
912 Canal Dr.
Chesapeake, VA 23323
Owner/Proprietor: Kenyatta
Ingram
Phone: 929-445-7427
Email: info@richesinreading.com
Opened in: 2015
Last updated: 2017-01-04 (171)

126 – <u>Urban Moon Books: The
Indie Author Outlet</u>
Chesapeake Square Mall, 4200
Portsmouth Blvd
Chesapeake, VA 23321
Owner/Proprietor: Fanita
Pendleton
Phone: 757-465-3858
Email:
urbanmoonbooksandmore@gmail.com
Opened in: 2016
Last updated: 2016-05-26 (167)

127 – <u>Books and Crannies</u>
50 E Church St Ste 4

Martinsville, VA 24112
Owner/Proprietor: DeShanta
Hairston
Phone: 276-403-4380
Email:
staff@booksandcranniesva.com
Opened in: 2016
Last updated: 2020-06-24 (219)

128 – House of Consciousness
633 West 35th Street
Norfolk, VA 23508
Owner/Proprietor:
Phone: 757-314-1943
Email: hocbulletin@gmail.com
Opened in: 1986
Last updated: 2015-03-17 (137)

129 – Timbuktu Bookstore
3601 East Ocean View Avenue,
Unit C.
Norfolk, VA 23518
Owner/Proprietor: Bro. Furqaan
S. Ali
Phone: 757-374-4591
Email:
Opened in: 2003
Last updated: 2014-04-06 (116)

130 – Positive Vibes
6220 B Indian River Rd.
Virginia Beach, VA 23464
Owner/Proprietor: A Partnership
Phone: 757-523-1399
Email:
Opened in: 1992

Brunches- Black Brunches around the world in black restaurants

Alabama

Brick and Spoon
3662 Airport Blvd # A, Mobile, AL 36608

Alaska

Roscoe's Catfish and Barbeque
120 E 6th Ave, Anchorage, AK 99501

Arizona

Lo-Lo's Chicken and Waffles
3133 N Scottsdale Rd, Scottsdale, AZ 85251
1220 S Central Ave, Phoenix, AZ 85003
366 N Gilbert Rd, Gilbert, AZ 85234

Arkansas

Ceci's Chicken N Waffles
1600 Dave Ward Dr, Conway, AR 72034

California

Brown Sugar Kitchen
2295 Broadway, Oakland, CA 94612

Colorado

Intersections Coffee
8241 Northfield Blvd, Denver, CO 80216

Connecticut

Craig's Kitchen
13 W Main St, Vernon, CT 06066

Delaware

Celebrations on Market
 340 S Market St, Wilmington, DE 19801

Florida

Spoons Grill
3987 NW 19th St, Lauderdale Lakes, FL 33311

Georgia

Spice House Cascade
2247 Cascade Rd SW, Atlanta, GA 30311

Hawaii

Rebel Kitchen
79-7399 Hawaii Belt Rd, Kealakekua, HI 96750

Idaho

Kibroms Ethiopian and Eritrean Cuisine

3506 W State St, Boise, ID
83703

Illinois

Batter and Berries
2748 N Lincoln Ave, Chicago, IL
60614

Indiana

Maxines Chicken and Waffles
132 N East St, Indianapolis, IN
46204

Iowa

SugaPeach Chicken and Fish
Fry
650 Pacha Pkwy # 1, North
Liberty, IA 52317

Kansas

Jones BBQ
6706 Kaw Dr, Kansas City, KS
66111

Kentucky

Shirley Mae's Café
802 S Clay St, Louisville, KY
40203

Louisiana

Lil Dizzy's Cafe
1500 Esplanade Ave, New
Orleans, LA 70116

Maine

Red Sea
30 Washington Ave, Portland,
ME 04101

Maryland

Georgia Peach
7165 Security Blvd, Windsor Mill,
MD 21244

Massachusetts

Daryl's Corner Bar
604 Columbus Ave, Boston, MA
02118

Michigan

Sweet Magnolias
29221 Northwestern Hwy,
Southfield, MI 48034

Minnesota

Breaking Bread Café
1210 W Broadway Ave,
Minneapolis, MN 55411

Mississippi

Alma Jean's Southern Kookin
122 Norfleet Dr, Senatobia, MS
38668

Missouri

Peach Tree Cafe
2128 E 12th St, Kansas City, MO
64127

Montana

The Sassy Biscuit
115 N 29th St, Billings, MT
59101

Nebraska

Quick Bites Soul Food
105 W Mission Ave, Bellevue,
NE 68005

Nevada

Gritz Café
1911 Stella Lake St #150, Las
Vegas, NV 89106

New Hampshire

Sassy Biscuit
104 Washington St Ste. 100,
Dover, NH 03820

New Jersey

The Soul Food Factory
431 Main St, East Orange, NJ
07018

New Mexico

Jambo Café:
2010 Cerrillos Rd #2010, Santa
Fe, NM 87505

New York

SoCo

509 Myrtle Ave, Brooklyn, NY
11205

North Carolina

Stephanies
2347 Randleman Rd,
Greensboro, NC 27406

North Dakota

Liberian Merry Go Round
Restaurant
855 45th St S, Fargo, ND 58103

Ohio

Super Chef's
1344 Cherry Bottom Rd,
Gahanna, OH 43230

Oklahoma

Waffle That
2115 M.L.K. Jr. Blvd. Tulsa, OK
74106

Oregon

Fish Fusion
5800 NE Martin Luther King Jr
Blvd, Portland, OR 97211

Pennsylvania

Rose Petals Café
8120 Old York Rd, Elkins Park,
PA 19027

Rhode Island

Monte Cara Restaurant
532 Lonsdale Ave, Pawtucket,
RI 02860

South Carolina

Kiki's Chicken and Waffles
7001 Parklane Rd, Columbia,
SC 29223

South Dakota

Swamp Daddy's Cajun Kitchen
421 N Phillips Ave, Sioux Falls,
SD 57104

Tennessee

99 cents soul food
414 S Main St, Memphis, TN
38103-4441

Texas

The Breakfast Klub
3711 Travis St, Houston, TX
77002

Utah

Joes Cafe
1126 State St, Orem, UT 84097

Vermont

Kismayo Kitchen
505 Riverside Ave Burlington,
VT 05401

Virginia
Mango Mangeaux
33 E Mellen St, Hampton, VA
23663

Washington

Plum Vegan Bistro
1429 12th Ave, Seattle, WA
98122

West Virginia

Sumthin Good Soul Food
4837 MacCorkle Ave SW, South
Charleston, WV 25309

Wisconsin

Coffee Makes You Black
2803 N Teutonia Ave,
Milwaukee, WI 53206

Wyoming

Simply Soul
6207 Missile Dr, Cheyenne, WY
82005

Washington, D.C.

Florida Avenue Grill
1100 Florida Ave NW,
Washington, DC 20009

International Brunch

Amsterdam

Water & Brood
Nieuwe Kerkstraat 84, 1018 EC
Amsterdam, Netherlands

Japan

Soul Food House
Japan, 〒106-0045 Tokyo,
Minato City, Azabujuban, 2
Chome-8-10 Ｐａｔｉｏ6F

London

Hip Hop Brunch London
https://www.hiphopbrunchldn.co
m/

Paris

Gumbo YAYA's
3 Rue Charles Robin, 75010
Paris, France

Black Food
Events-Mobile

Black Restaurant Week
https://blackrestaurantweeks.co
m/
Grits and biscuits
https://gritsandbiscuits.com/

Carnivals

Anguilla: Taking place in August, Anguilla's Carnival features boat racing, beach barbecues, and bandstands.

Antigua: Join much of Antigua's population in watching the brass and steel bands play in August.

Aruba: Held in the traditional season (around February), Aruba's includes a night parade and the crowning of royalty.

Bahamas: "Junkanoo," as it's called here, happens every year on Boxing Day and New Year's Day.

Barbados: Barbados holds "Crop Over" in August.

Bermuda: Hero Weekend takes place in June

Bonaire: Come witness the Old Mask Parade and the Burning of King Momo in February.

British Virgin Islands: Folks in the British Virgin Islands call it the "Emancipation Festival" and it's held from the end of July to the beginning of August.

Cayman Islands: "Batabano" is a colorful celebration of community spirit held the first week of May in George Town.

Cuba: Cuba's Carnival is held in July and features street performances by cultural dancers called comparsas.

Curacao: Taking place during the traditional Lent season, this one includes a certain kind of Carnival music called "Tumba."

Dominica: Dominica holds a two-day block party called the Street Jump Up during Lent season.

Dominican Republic: Expect elaborate masks and multi-town celebrations in February.

Grenada: "Spicemas" or "August Mas" is an exuberant festival that takes place every August.

Guadeloupe: Guadeloupe's Carnival is famous for its dance marathons and competitions.

Haiti: Haitians celebrate with a kind of festival music called Rara and a variety of Creole celebrations, all held during the traditional Lent period.

Jamaica: Jamaica's "Bacchanal" takes place in April with several vibrant parades.

50

London; London's "Notitng Hill" Carnival takes place in September

Martinique: Martinique hosts the burning of "Vaval the Carnival King" during February.

Miami, Florida: Carnival takes place in October

Montserrat: Carnival here is all about beauty pageants and masqueraders, held in December.

Puerto Rico: The quintessential Puerto Rican vejigante masks will be ever-present at this festival, held from January to February.

Saba: Carnival Monday (the last Monday in July) is a public holiday in Saba. It's when the locals celebrate the "Old Caribbean."

St. Eustatius: On the last week of July, St. Eustatius celebrates with dancing, beauty contests, food, and drinking.

St. Barts: This Mardi Gras-like festival, leading up to Ash Wednesday, features a pajama parade.

St. Kitts and Nevis: "Sugar Mas" ("Sugar Cup" in English) is like a cocktail party that lasts from November to January.

St. Lucia: St. Lucia's Carnival is held in July and features a Parade of the Bands.

St. Martin/Maarten: Held during Lent and in April, respectively, these celebrations include balloon parades and light parades.

St. Vincent and the Grenadines: "Vincy Mas" is held from June to July, but J'Ouvert (one long, 24-hour party) is the main event.

Toronto: " Caribana" takes place in August

Trinidad and Tobago: This is the biggest and most well-known Carnival in the Caribbean, held during the traditional Mardi Gras season.

Turks and Caicos: Like the Bahamas, Turks and Caicos also celebrate "Junkanoo" in December and January.

U.S. Virgin Islands: St. Croix's celebration is held in December and January, while the party in St. Thomas is held in April.

Colleges

Historically Black Colleges and Universities (HBCU's)

ALABAMA

Alabama A&M University
Alabama State University
Bishop State Community College
C.A. Fredd Campus of Shelton State Community College
Concordia College Selma
Gadsden State Community College
J. F. Drake Technical College
Lawson State Community College
Miles College
Oakwood College
Selma University
Stillman College
Talladega College
Trenholm State Technical College
Tuskegee University

ARKANSAS

Arkansas Baptist College
Philander Smith College
Shorter College
University of Arkansas at Pine Bluff

DELAWARE

Delaware State University

DISTRICT OF COLUMBIA

Howard University
University of the District of Columbia

FLORIDA

Bethune-Cookman University
Edward Waters College
Florida A&M University
Florida Memorial University

GEORGIA

Albany State University
Clark Atlanta University
Fort Valley State University
Interdenominational Theological Center
Morehouse College
Morehouse School of Medicine
Morris Brown College
Paine College
Savannah State University
Spelman College

KENTUCKY

Kentucky State University

LOUISIANA

Dillard University
Grambling State University
Southern University and A&M College
Southern University at New Orleans
Southern University at Shreveport

Xavier University of Louisiana

MARYLAND

Bowie State University
Coppin State University
Morgan State University
University of Maryland, Eastern
Shore

MICHIGAN

Lewis College of Business

MISSISSIPPI

Alcorn State University
Coahoma Community College
Hinds Community College
Jackson State University
Mississippi Valley State
University
Rust College
Tougaloo College

MISSOURI

Harris-Stowe State University
Lincoln University of Missouri

NORTH CAROLINA

Barber-Scotia College
Bennett College
Elizabeth City State University
Fayetteville State University
Johnson C. Smith University
Livingstone College
North Carolina A&T State
University
North Carolina Central University

St. Augustine's College
Shaw University
Winston Salem State University

OHIO

Central State University
Wilberforce University

OKLAHOMA

Langston University

PENNSYLVANIA

Cheyney University of
Pennsylvania
Lincoln University

SOUTH CAROLINA

Allen University
Benedict College
Claflin University
Clinton Junior College
Denmark Technical College
Morris College
South Carolina State University
Voorhees College

TENNESSEE

American Baptist College
Fisk University
Knoxville College
Lane College
LeMoyne-Owen College
Meharry Medical College
Tennessee State University

TEXAS

Huston-Tillotson University
Jarvis Christian College
Paul Quinn College
Prairie View A&M University
Saint Philip's College
Southwestern Christian College
Texas College
Texas Southern University
Wiley College

VIRGINIA

Hampton University
Norfolk State University
Virginia State University
Virginia Union University
Virginia University of Lynchburg

WEST VIRGINIA

Bluefield State College
West Virginia State University

U.S. VIRGIN ISLANDS

University of the Virgin Islands

HBCU'S with tourism programs raising the next generation of travel leaders!.

Bethune Cookman University

Cheyney University of Pennsylvania

Coahoma Community College

Delaware State University

Grambling State University

Hampton University

Howard University

Morgan State University

North Carolina Central University

St Philip's College

Tougaloo College

Tuskegee University

University of Maryland Eastern Shore

University of The District of Columbia

Virginia State University

Credit Unions

1. 1st Choice Credit Union-
Georgia
Branches: Auburn
Avenue Administrative
Office (Atlanta, Ga.) and
Grady Memorial Hospital
(Atlanta, Ga.)
ATMs: Crestview Health
& Rehabilitation Center
(Atlanta, Ga.) and Ponce
De Leon Center (Atlanta,
Ga.)
2. Alamerica Bank-
Alabama
Branches: The
Alamerica Bank Building
(Birmingham,
Ala.)ATMs: N/A
3. Broadway Federal Bank-
California
Branches: Mid-Wilshire
Branch (Los Angeles,
Calif.), Inglewood
Branch (Inglewood,
Calif.), and Exposition
Park Branch (Los
Angeles, Calif.)
ATMs: Part of the
MoneyPass network
4. Brookland Federal
Credit Union-South
Carolina
Branches: Brookland
Federal Credit Union
(West Columbia, S.C.)
ATMs: N/A
5. Carver Federal Savings
Bank- New York

Branches: Atlantic
Terminal Branch
(Brooklyn, N.Y.),
Bedford-Stuyvesant -
Restoration Plaza
Branch (Brooklyn, N.Y.),
Crown Heights Branch
(Brooklyn, N.Y.),
Flatbush Branch
(Brooklyn, N.Y.), and St
Albans Branch
(Jamaica, N.Y.), 125th
Street Branch (New York
City, N.Y.), and Malcolm
X Boulevard Branch
(New York City, N.Y.)
ATMs: Atlantic Terminal
Shopping Mall (2)
(Brooklyn, N.Y.) and
ATM Banking Center
(Brooklyn, N.Y.)
6. Carver State Bank-
Georgia
Branches: Main Office
(Savannah, Ga.) and
Skidaway Branch
(Savannah, Ga.)
ATMs: Main Office
(Savannah, Ga.),
Skidaway Branch
(Savannah, Ga.), and
Hilton Head International
Airport (Savannah, Ga.)
7. Citizens Bank-
Tennessee
Branches: Memphis
Winchester Road
Branch (Memphis,
Tenn.) and Main Office
(Nashville, Tenn.)

ATMs: Main Office
(Nashville, Tenn.

8. Citizens Trust Bank-
Alabama and Georgia
Branches: Birmingham
(Birmingham, Ala.),
Eutaw Branch (Eutaw,
Ala.), Cascade Branch
(Atlanta, Ga.), Corporate
Headquarters (Atlanta,
Ga.), Westside Branch
(Atlanta, Ga.), East Point
Branch (East Point,
Ga.), and Rockbridge
Branch (Stone Mountain,
Ga.)23
ATMs: Castleberry Inn
ATM (Atlanta, Ga.),
Westside ATM (Atlanta,
Ga.), South Dekalb Mall
ATM (Decatur, Ga.),
Lithonia ATM (Lithonia,
Ga.), Rockbridge Plaza
ATM (Stone Mountain,
Ga.), Stone Mountain
ATM (Stone Mountain,
Ga.), and Panola ATM
(Stonecrest, Ga.

9. Columbia Savings &
Loan- Wisconsin
Branches: Columbia
Savings & Loan
Association (Milwaukee,
Wis.)
ATMs: N/A

10. Commonwealth National
Bank
Branches: Main Office
Branch (Mobile, Ala.)
and Crichton Branch
(Mobile, Ala.)ATMs:

Main Office Branch
(Mobile, Ala.), Crichton
Branch (Mobile, Ala.),
any Publix Super Market
ATM, and any PNC
Bank ATM126

11. Community Owned
Federal Credit Union-
South Carolina
Branches: Community
Owned Federal Credit
Union (Charleston,
S.C.)65
ATMs: N/A

12. Credit Union of Atlanta-
Georgia
Branches: Main Office
(Atlanta, Ga.) and Pryor
Street Lending Center
(Atlanta, Ga.)ATMs:
Atlanta Detention Center
(Atlanta, Ga.), Atlanta
Public Safety Annex
(Atlanta, Ga.), Credit
Union of Atlanta
(Atlanta, Ga.), Pryor
Street Lending Center
(Atlanta, Ga.), in addition
to any ATMs in the
MoneyPass and STAR
networks

13. Faith Community United
Credit Union-Ohio
Branches: Faith
Community United
Credit Union (Cleveland,
Ohio)
ATMs: N/A

14. Faith Cooperative Credit
Union-Texas

Branches: Administrative
Offices (Dallas, Texas)
ATMs: One located
"near the Banquet Hall"
15. FAMU Federal Credit
Union-Florida
Branches: Office
(Tallahassee, Fla.)
ATMs: One located in
the "first drive-thru lane"
as well as any ATMs
that are part of the
American Express,
CULIANCE, The
Exchange, Honors,
Member Access, Plus,
Presto, Publix, Walmart,
and "other Credit Unions
with the participating
listed networks"
16. First Independence
Bank- Michigan
Branches: Clinton
Township Branch
(Clinton Township,
Mich.), Main Office
Branch (Detroit, Mich.),
and Seven Mile Branch
(Detroit, Mich.)
ATMs: Garfield Branch
(Clinton Township,
Mich.), 1st Floor
International Building
(Detroit, Mich.), City
County Building (Detroit,
Mich.), Livernois
(Detroit, Mich.), and
Main Office Branch
(Detroit, Mich.), Seven
Mile Branch (Detroit,
Mich.), in addition to

"any nationwide ... Fifth
Third, TCF, or Chemical
Bank ATM ... in the
Metro Detroit area"
17. First Legacy Community
Credit Union-North
Carolina
Branches: First Legacy
Community Credit Union
(Charlotte, N.C.)
ATMs: Part of the CO-
OP/Covera ATM
network
18. First Security Bank-
Iowa
Branches: Aredale
(Aredale, Iowa), Charles
City Branch (Charles
City, Iowa), Dumont
Branch (Dumont, Iowa),
Hampton Branch
(Hampton, Iowa), Ionia
Branch (Ionia, Iowa),
Manly Branch (Manly,
Iowa), Marble Rock
Branch (Marble Rock,
Iowa), Nora Springs
Branch (Nora Springs,
Iowa), Riceville Branch
(Riceville, Iowa),
Rockford Branch
(Rockford, Iowa),
Rockwell Branch
(Rockwell, Iowa), Rudd
Branch (Rudd, Iowa),
and Thornton Branch
(Thornton, Iowa)
ATMs: Charles City
Branch (Charles City,
Iowa), Manly Branch
(Manly, Iowa), Marble

Rock Branch (Marble Rock, Iowa), Nora Springs Branch (Nora Springs, Iowa), Riceville Branch (Riceville, Iowa), Rockford Branch (Rockford, Iowa), Rockwell Branch (Rockwell, Iowa), and Thornton Branch (Thornton, Iowa)

19. GN Bank- Illinois Branches: Main Branch (Chicago, Ill.) and Chatham Office (Chicago, Ill.) ATMs: Main Branch (Chicago, Ill.) and Chatham Office (Chicago, Ill.), in addition to any ATMs in the STAR network.
20. Greater Kinston Credit Union- North Carolina Branches: Branch Office (Kinston, N.C.) ATMs: Part of the CashPoints network
21. Hill District Federal Credit Union- Pennsylvania Branches: Hill District Federal Credit Union (Pittsburgh, Pa.) ATMs: N/A
22. Hope Credit Union- Alabama, Arkansas, Louisiana, Mississippi, and Tennessee

Branches: Arba Street Branch (Montgomery, Ala.), McGehee Road Branch (Montgomery, Ala.), College Station Branch (College Station, Ark.), Little Rock Branch (Little Rock, Ark.), Pine Bluff Branch (Pine Bluff, Ark.), West Memphis Branch (West Memphis, Ark.), Central City Branch (New Orleans, La.), Elysian Fields Branch (New Orleans, La.), Michoud Assembly Facility Branch (New Orleans, La.), Mississippi Coast Branch (Biloxi, Miss.), Drew Branch (Drew, Miss.), Greenville Branch (Greenville, Miss.), Itta Bena Branch (Itta Bena, Miss.), Medical Mall Branch (Jackson, Miss.), University Boulevard Branch (Jackson, Miss.), Louisville Branch (Louisville, Miss.), Macon Branch (Macon, Miss.), Moorhead Branch (Moorhead, Miss.), Robinsonville Branch (Robinsonville, Miss.), Shaw Branch (Shaw, Miss.), Terry MS Branch (Terry, Miss.), Utica Branch (Utica, Miss.), West Point

Branch (West Point, Miss.), Jackson Branch (Jackson, Tenn.), Crosstown Branch (Memphis, Tenn.), Harvester Lane Branch (Memphis, Tenn.), Madison Avenue Branch (Memphis, Tenn.), and Ridgeway Branch (Memphis, Tenn.), in addition to any credit unions in the Shared Branching network.

23. ATMs: Pine Bluff Branch (Pine Bluff, Ark.), West Memphis Branch (West Memphis, Ark.), Central City Branch (New Orleans, La.), Elysian Fields Branch (New Orleans, La.), Mississippi Coast Branch (Biloxi, Miss.), Drew Branch (Drew, Miss.), Greenville Branch (Greenville, Miss.), Medical Mall Branch (Jackson, Miss.), University Boulevard Branch (Jackson, Miss.), Robinsonville Branch (Robinsonville, Miss.), Shaw Branch (Shaw, Miss.), Terry MS Branch (Terry, Miss.), Jackson Branch (Jackson, Tenn.), Harvester Lane Branch (Memphis, Tenn.), Madison Avenue Branch (Memphis,

Tenn.), and Ridgeway Branch (Memphis, Tenn.)

24. Howard University Employees Federal Credit Union- Washington D.C Branches: C B Powell Building (Washington D.C.) ATMs: Part of the CO-OP and CU Here networks

25. Industrial Bank- States: New Jersey, New York, and Washington D.C. Branches: Harlem Banking Center (New York City, N.Y.), Bergen Street Banking Center (Newark, N.J.), Halsey Street Banking Center (Newark, N.J.), Anacostia Gateway Banking Center (Washington D.C.), F Street Banking Center (Washington D.C.), Forestville Banking Center (Washington D.C.), Georgia Avenue Banking Center (Washington D.C.), J.H. Mitchell Banking Center (Washington D.C.), Oxon Hill Banking Center (Washington D.C.), and U Street Banking Center (Washington D.C.)

26. ATMs: Harlem Office (New York City, N.Y.), Bergen Street Office (Newark, N.J.), Halsey Street Office (Newark, N.J.), Anacostia Gateway Office (Washington D.C.), Ben's Chili Bowl (Washington D.C.), DC Court of Appeals (Washington D.C.), DC Superior Court (2) (Washington D.C.), F Street Office (Washington D.C.), Forestville Office (Washington D.C.), Georgia Avenue Office (Washington D.C.), J.H. Mitchell Office (Washington D.C.), Nationals Park (Washington D.C.), Oxon Hill Office (Washington D.C.), and U Street Office (Washington D.C.), in addition to any ATMs in the Allpoint network

27. Liberty Bank - Alabama, Illinois, Kansas, Kentucky, Louisiana, Michigan, Mississippi, and Missouri Branches: Montgomery Liberty Bank (Montgomery, Ala.), Tuskegee Liberty Bank (Tuskegee, Ala.), Liberty Bank Forest Park (Forest Park, Ill.), Kansas City Liberty Bank (Kansas City, Kan.), Louisville Liberty Bank (Louisville, Ky.), Southdowns Liberty Bank (Baton Rouge, La.), Southern Heights Liberty Bank (Baton Rouge, La.), Canal Street Liberty Bank (New Orleans, La.), Crowder Blvd Liberty Bank (New Orleans, La.), Franklin Ave Liberty Bank (New Orleans, La.), General DeGaulle Liberty Bank (New Orleans, La.), Gentilly Blvd Liberty Bank (New Orleans, La.), Woodward Ave Liberty Bank (Detroit, Mich.), Jackson Liberty Bank (Jackson, Miss.), and Kansas City Liberty Bank (Kansas City, Mo.)

28. ATMs: Montgomery Liberty Bank (Montgomery, Ala.), Tuskegee Liberty Bank (Tuskegee, Ala.), Liberty Bank Forest Park (Forest Park, Ill.), 4850 State Street (Kansas City, Kan.), Southdowns Liberty Bank (Baton Rouge, La.), Southern Heights Liberty Bank (Baton Rouge, La.), 910-B Decatur Street (New Orleans, La.), 2800

Gravier Street (New Orleans, La.), American Can (New Orleans, La.), Canal Street Liberty Bank (New Orleans, La.), City Hall (New Orleans, La.), Crowder Blvd Liberty Bank (New Orleans, La.), Dillard - Rosenwald Hall (New Orleans, La.), Franklin Rouses (New Orleans, La.), French Market (New Orleans, La.), General DeGaulle Liberty Bank (New Orleans, La.), Gentilly Blvd Liberty Bank (New Orleans, La.), Lafon Nursing Facility (New Orleans, La.), Lockheed Martin Buildings 102 & 350 (New Orleans, La.), Orleans Sheriff (New Orleans, La.), Xavier University (2) (New Orleans, La.), Jackson Evers International Airport (Jackson, Miss.), Jackson Liberty Bank (Jackson, Miss.), Student Center (Jackson, Miss.), Tougaloo College (Jackson, Miss.), and Union Station (Jackson, Miss.)

29. Mechanics & Farmers Bank- North Carolina Branches: Charlotte (Charlotte, N.C.), Corporate Headquarters (Durham, N.C.), Durham Branch – Durham-Chapel Hill Boulevard (Durham, N.C.), Greensboro (Greensboro, N.C.), Raleigh Branch – Rock Quarry Road (Raleigh, N.C.), Winston-Salem (Winston-Salem, N.C.) ATMs: Durham Branch (Durham, N.C.) and Raleigh Branch – East Hargett Street (Raleigh, N.C.)

30. Metro Bank - Alabama Branches: Ashville Office (Ashville, Ala.), Heflin Office (Heflin, Ala.), Lincoln Office (Lincoln, Ala.), Moody Office (Moody, Ala.), Main Office (Pell City, Ala.), North Office (Pell City, Ala.), South Office (Pell City, Ala.), Ragland Office (Ragland, Ala.), Southside Office (Southside, Ala.) ATMs: Ashville Office (Ashville, Ala.), Heflin Office (Heflin, Ala.), Lincoln Office (Lincoln, Ala.), Main Office (Pell City, Ala.), Moody Office (Moody, Ala.), North Office (Pell City, Ala.), Odenville ATM (Odenville, Ala.) South Office (Pell City, Ala.),

Ragland Office
(Ragland, Ala.),
Southside Office
(Southside, Ala.)

31. Mount Olive Baptist
Church Federal Credit
Union - Texas
Branches: Mount Olive
Baptist Church FCU
(Dallas, Texas)
ATMs: N/A

32. Oak Cliff Christian
Federal Credit Union-
Texas
Branches: Oak Cliff
Christian FCU (Dallas, Texas)
ATMs: N/A

33. Omega Psi Phi
Fraternity Federal Credit
Union-Georgia
Branches: Omega Psi
Phi Fraternity Federal
Credit Union c/o CAMO
(Toccoa, Ga.) ATMs:
N/A

34. OneUnited Bank -
California, Florida, and
Massachusetts
Branches: Compton
Branch (Coming Soon)
(Compton, Cali.),
Corporate Office and
Crenshaw Branch (Los
Angeles, Cali.), Miami
Branch (Miami, Fla.),
Corporate Headquarters
(Boston, Mass.), and
Roxbury Branch
(Roxbury, Mass.)
ATMs: Part of the
MoneyPass network

35. OPTUS Bank-South
Carolina
Branches: Main Branch
(Columbia, S.C.)
ATMs: Beltline Branch
(Columbia, S.C.),
Corporate Office
(Columbia, S.C.), Main
Branch (Columbia, S.C.)

36. South Side Community
Federal Credit Union-
Illinois
Branches: South Side
Community Federal
Credit Union (Chicago,
Ill.)40
ATMs: N/A

37. Southern Teachers &
Parents Federal Credit
Union-Louisiana
Branches: Main Office
(Baton Rouge, La.) and
Lafeda Branch
(Thibodaux, La.)
ATMs: Part of the CU
Alliance network

38. St. Louis Community
Credit Union-Missouri
Branches: Ferguson
Branch (Ferguson, Mo.),
Florissant Branch
(Florissant, Mo.), Flower
Valley Branch
(Florissant, Mo.),
Pagedale Branch
(Pagedale, Mo.),
Richmond Heights
(Richmond Heights,
Mo.), St. John Branch
(St. John), Benton Park
Branch (St. Louis, Mo.),

Gateway Branch (St. Louis, Mo.), Grace Hill (St. Louis, Mo.), Jennings Branch (St. Louis, Mo.), LifeWise STL (St. Louis, Mo.), Midtown Branch (St. Louis, Mo.), South City (St. Louis, Mo.), Southtown Branch (St. Louis, Mo.), Sullivan Branch (St. Louis, Mo.), University City (University City, Mo.), MET Center (Wellston, Mo.) ATMs: Part of the CO-OP network

39. The Harbor Bank of Maryland
Branches: Inner Harbor East Office (Baltimore, Md.), Main Office (Baltimore, Md.), Pimlico Office (Baltimore, Md.), Research Park Office (Baltimore, Md.), The Harbor Science & Technology Park East Branch (Baltimore, Md.), Randallstown Office (Randallstown, Md.), and Silver Spring (Silver Spring, Md.)
ATMs: Inner Harbor East Office (Baltimore, Md.), Main Office (Baltimore, Md.), Pimlico Office (Baltimore, Md.), Research Park Office (Baltimore, Md.), The Harbor Science & Technology Park East Branch (Baltimore, Md.), Randallstown Office (Randallstown, Md.), and Silver Spring (Silver Spring, Md.), in addition to any ATMS in the AllPoint network

40. Toledo Urban Federal Credit Union-Ohio
Branches: Nexus Building (Toledo, Ohio) and Toledo Urban Federal Credit Union (Toledo, Ohio) ATMs: N/A

41. Tri-State Bank-Tennessee
Branches: Whitehaven (Memphis, Tenn.)
ATMs: Whitehaven (Memphis, Tenn.) and any ATMs in the Money Tower network

42. United Bank of Philadelphia - Pennsylvania
Branches: Center City (Philadelphia, Pa.) and Progress Plaza (Philadelphia, Pa.)
ATMs: C-Town Supermarket (Philadelphia, Pa.), City Hall (Philadelphia, Pa.), Criminal Justice Center (Philadelphia, Pa.), Masjidullah Inc. (Philadelphia, Pa.), Philadelphia Traffic Court (Philadelphia,

Pa.), Police Districts
(Philadelphia, Pa.),
Revolutions at Penn
Treaty (Philadelphia,
Pa.), The Fillmore-
Philadelphia
(Philadelphia, Pa.), and
West Philadelphia
(Philadelphia, Pa.)

43. Unity National Bank -
Georgia and Texas
Branches: Atlanta
(Atlanta, Ga.) Blodgett
(Houston, Texas), and
Fort Bend (Missouri City,
Texas)
ATMs: Atlanta (Atlanta,
Ga.) Blodgett (Houston,
Texas), and Fort Bend
(Missouri City, Texas), in
addition to any ATMs in
the Select network

44. Urban Upbound Federal
Credit Union-New York
Branches: Urban
Upbound Federal Credit
Union (Long Island City,
N.Y.)
ATMs: N/A

45. Virginia State University
Federal Credit Union-
Virginia
Branches: Virginia State
University Federal Credit
Union (South
Chesterfield, Va.)
ATMs: Virginia State
University Federal Credit
Union (South
Chesterfield, Va.)

Cruises

http://www.blackcruiseweek.com/

1. Tom Joyner Fantastic Voyage Cruise

"Party with a Purpose" in the Caribbean
PORTS: Miami, St. Thomas, San Juan and Grand Turk

2.Festival At Sea

Oldest black cruise operator; cruise with over 2000 black folk
PORTS: Fort Lauderdale, San Juan, Tortola, Punta Cana and Key West

3. Abundant Life Singles Cruise

Christian cruise for singles
PORTS: Miami, Ocho Rios and Grand Cayman Island

4.Grown and Sexy Cruise

Calls itself the the Biggest Party at Sea
PORTS: Aruba, Bonaire, Curacao and St. Maarten

5.Huddle on the Sea Cruise

Join sexy, accomplished, beautiful people at sea
PORTS:Miami, Dominican Republic, St. Thomas, San Juan and Grand Turk

6.Capital Super Cruise

A spin-off from the Capital Jazz Concert
PORTS:Belize City, Haiti, Honduras and Cozumel

7.NPN Cruise

Cruises tailored to continuing education for professionals, primarily medical
PORTS: Miami, Havana and Cozumel

8.Oprah Cruise

Join Oprah Winfrey, Gayle King and friends for all things Oprah
PORTS: Fort Lauderdale and Half Moon Cay, Bahamas

9.Black Marriage Cruise

Chilling with with the happily married couples in exotic locations
PORTS: Miami, Grand Cayman, Mahogany Bay, Belize and Cozumel

10.Uber Soca Cruise

<u>The Largest Soca Festival at Sea!</u>
PORTS: Belize -Costa Maya, Mexico

Cycling Clubs

http://blackcyclingclubs.com/
National Brotherhood of Cyclists

Arkansas

1. Major Taylor Cycling Club of Little Rock

California

1. Bel-Cal Cycling Club-
2. Dockriders
3. Major Motion Cycling Club
4. Major Taylor Cycling Club of San Diego
5. Oakland Yellow Jackets
6. Red Bike & Green

Colorado

1. Major Taylor Cycling Club of Denver

DC – Maryland – Virginia

1. Artemis Racing
2. Baltimore Metro Wheelers Cycling Club
3. Black Ski DC
4. Brother to Brother Sister to Sister United

Georgia

1. Metro Atlanta Cycling Club
2. Velo Atlanta

Illinois

1. Major Taylor Cycling Club of Chicago

Michigan

1. Metro Detroit Cycling Club

Minnesota

1. Major Taylor Cycling Club Minnesota

Missouri

1. Hill Street Spinners
2. Major Taylor Cycling Club Ironriders
3. Major Taylor Cycling Club of New Jersey
4. Major Taylor Cycling Club of NY/NJ

North Carolina

1. Cannonballs Cycling Team

Ohio

1. Major Taylor Cycling Club of Columbus
2. Major Taylor Cycling Club of Dayton

Pennsylvania

1. Bikin Blazers
2. Pittsburgh Major Taylor Cycling Club

Tennessee

1. Major Momentum Cycling Club

Texas

1. D.R.A.F.T Cycling Club
2. Major Taylor Cycling Club of Austin
3. Major Velocity Cycling

Washington

1. Soul Sistas

Motocycle Clubs

https://www.blackmotorcycleclub
s.us/
Over 100

Dispensaries/Cannabis

Cannabis Tours
https://cannabistours.com/
Alaska, California, Colorado, DC

North America

California

Blunts and Moore
701 66th Ave suite b,
Oakland, CA 94621

California Cannabis Melrose
654 N MANHATTAN PL,
LOS ANGELES, CA 90004
California Street Cannabis
1398 California Street,
San Francisco, CA 94109

Mankind Cannabis
7128 Miramar Rd,
San Diego, CA 92121

Colorado

Simply Pure
2000 W 32nd Ave,
Denver, CO 80211
Massachusettes

Pure Oasis
430 Blue Hill Ave Boston,
MA 02121

Maryland

Mary and Main

8801 Hampton Mall Dr N,
Capitol Heights, MD 20743

Oklahoma

Aquila Dispensary
501 12th Ave NW,
Ardmore, OK 73401

Oregon

Green Hop
5515 NE 16TH AVE,
PORTLAND, OR 97211

Elev8cannabis
Illinois, Massachusetts, Oregon
https://www.elev8cannabis.com/

Washington

Kush 21
17730 Ambaum Blvd
S Seattle, WA 98148

Washington D.C.

Metropolitan Wellness Center
409 8th St SE #201,
Washington, DC 20003

Europe

Netherlands

African Black Star
Rozengracht 1-A, 1016 LP
Amsterdam, Netherlands

Distilleries/Wineries/Alcohol Brands

Association of African American
Vitners
https://www.aaavintners.org/

Distilleries

Anteel Tequila
Co-owned by Nayana Ferguson,
Don Ferguson and Mike
Rowoldt. Michigan

Black Momma Vodka
The line-up of vodkas from this
company, helmed by
CEO/President Vanessa Braxton
(sister-in-law to singer/songwriter
Toni Braxton)

Brough Brothers
Owned by brothers Victor,
Christian and Bryson Yarbrough.
Kentucky

Carbonadi Vodka
Ricky Miller III . Italy

Du Nord Craft Spirits
Owned by Chris Montana, also
the president of the American
Craft Spirits Association.

Fresh Bourbon
Sean Edwards . Kentucky
Loft + Bear
Paul Ryan Elliot. California

Revel Spirits
CEO/founder Micah McFarlane.
Mexico

Ten to One Rum
Marc Farrell . Carribean

Uncle Nearest
Fawn Weaver. Tennessee

Wineries

North America

Abbey Creek Vineyard: Oregon
Alexis George Wines: California
Amour Genéve: Wine
Bodkin Wines: California
Brown Estate:California
Charles Wine Company: Wine
Charles Woodson Intercept:
California
Corner 103: California
Darjean Jones Wines: Wine
Davidson Wine Co.: North
Carolina.
Davine Wines: Spirits
Domaine Curry:Wine
Earl Stevens Selections: Wine
and Tequila
ENAT Winery: California
Esrever Wines: New York
Eunice Chiweshe Goldstein
Winery: Oregon
FLO Wine: Wine
Fog Crest Vineyard: Wine
Free Range Flower Winery:
Oakland
Frichette Winery: Washington
Indigené Cellars: California

J. Moss Wines:California
Jenny Dawn Cellars: Kansas
La Fête du Rosé: Wine
Le Loup Gris:California
L'Objet Noir: California
Longevity Wines: California
Love Cork Screw: Illinois
LVE Collection: Wine
L'Tonya Renee Red Blend:
Markell-Bani: Ohio
Maison Noir Wines: Oregon
Sommelier and Wine
McBride Sisters: Wines
Michael Rose Cellars: California
MYX Fusions: Wine
Okapi Wines: California
Ole' Orleans Wines: New
Orleans
P. Harrell Wines: California
Sapiens: Non alcoholic wine
Shoe Crazy Wine Wine
Simply Love Wines: Wine
Sip & Share Wines: Vegan Wine
Sosabe Wines: Wine
Stoney Wines: Wine with a
Cause
Stover Oaks Vineyard &
Winery:California
Stuyvesant Champagne:
Brooklyn inspired Champagne
Taste Collection Cellars:
California
Theopolis Vineyards: California
Tympany Vineyards: California
Vina Sympatica: Sparkling
Wines
Virgo Cellars: California
Vision Cellars: California
Wade Cellars: Wine(California,
Dwayne Wade)
Wachira Wines: California

Wandering Wines: Wine(Florida)
Wifey Brands: Sparkling Wines
Zafa Wines: Wine(Vermont and
Texas)

France

Armand de Brignac: Champagne
(France, Jay Z)
Cheurlin Champagne:
Champagne (Isaiah Thomas)
Marie Césaire: Champagne

Germany

Edelheiss Wine: Wine

Italy

Il Palazzone: Wine

Kenya

Saikeri Estate: Wine

South Africa

Adama Wines: Wine
Aslina Wines: Wine
Bayede: Wine (Cape winelands)
Blouvlei Wines: Wine
Botébo Wines: Wine
Cape Dreams: Biodiversity Wine
Carmen Stevens Wines: Naked
Wines
Compagniesdrift: 3 Wine families
Doornkraal Wines: The
Doornkraal farm
Earthbound: Fairtrade Wine
Epicuriean Wine: Wine
Fairvalley: Fair Trade Wine

Five's Reserve: Wine
House of Mandela: Wine
Imvula Wines: Wine (Western
Cape)
Inkosi Wines: Wine
J9 Wines: Wine (Western Cape)
Koni Wines: Wine (South Africa)
Koopmanskloof: Wine , Fair
Trade
Kumusha Wines: Wine
(Zimbabwe)
La RicMal: Sustainable Wine
Land of Hope: Wine education
Lathithá Wines: Wine estate
Libby's Pride: Wine
Liz Ogumbo Wines: Wine
(Kenya)
M'Hudi: Wine (South Africa)
Magna Carta Wines: Wine
Mosi Wines: Wine Zimbabwe
PaardenKloof: Wine
Paul Roos Wine: Wine
education
Sena Wines: Wine
Ses'Fikile: Wine (Cape
Winelands.)
Seven Sisters: Wine
Siwela Wines: Sparkling
(Western Cape)
Solms-Delta: Winery
Son of the Soil Wines: Wine
Tesselaarsdal Wines: Wine
The Bridge of Hope Wines: Wine
Thembi Wines: Wine , Fairtrade
Thokozani: Wine
Women in Wine: Wine
empowerment

Festivals

Afrochella
Accra, Ghana
Afrocella.com

Afro Nation
Portugal, Puerto Rico, & Ghana
Afronation.com

Afro Punk
Paris, France; Brooklyn, New York; Johannesburg, South Africa
https://afropunk.com/

Chale Wote Street Fest
Accra, Ghana
http://accradotaltradio.com/chale-wote-street-art-festival/

Curl Fest
New York, New York ; Atlanta, Georgia, USA
Curlfest.com

Dak'Art
Dakar, Senegal

Essence Festival
New Orleans , Louisian
Essence.com

One Music Fest
Atlanta, Georgia, USA
onemusicfest.com

Something in the Water
Virginia Beach, Virginia, USA.
https://somethinginthewater.com/

Yam Festival
London England
https://yamcarnival.com/

Flight Attendants

Black Flight Attendants of
America
http://www.blackflightattendantso
famerica.org/

Food Guides and apps

Eat Black Owned
www.eatblackowned.com

Eat Okra App
https://www.eatokra.com/
Black and Mobile- Delivery App
https://www.blackandmobile.com
/

Black History Tours (International)-

Black Heritage Tours- Amsterdam
www.blackheritagetours.com

Black History Walks- London
www.blackhistorywalks.co.uk

African Lisbon Tours- Portugal
https://africanlisbontour.com/

Experience Real Cartagena- Colombia
experiencerealcartagena.com

Black Paris Tour- Paris
www.blackparistour.com

Le Paris Noir- Paris
http://www.blackpariswalks.com/

Afro Tours Bahia- Brazil
https://www.toursbylocals.com/SalvadorBahiaPrivateAfroHeritage

Historical Landmarks

Google Map of Black History Landmarks and Monuments to visit.Provided by Adrienne.
https://goo.gl/maps/vNR4VT7hN nqr21bx5

Museums

A. Philip Randolph Pullman Porter Museum- Chicago, IL

African American Civil War Memorial Museum-Washington D.C.

African-American Research Library and Cultural Center- Fort Lauderdale FL.

African American Firefighter Museum-Los Angeles, CA

African American Multicultural Museum-Scottsdale, AZ

African American Museum-Dallas, TX

African American Museum and Library- Oakland, CA

African American Museum in Cleveland - Cleveland, OH

African American Museum in Philadelphia- Philadelphia , PA

African American Museum of Iowa- Cedar Rapids, IO

African American Museum of Nassau County- Hempstead, NY

African American Museum of the Arts- DeLand, Florida

African American Museum of Southern Illinois- Carbondale

Afro-American Historical and Cultural Society Museum, Jersey City, New Jersey

Alabama State Black Archives Research Center and Museum-Hunstville, AL

Alexandria Black History Museum- Alexandria, VA

America's Black Holocaust Museum- Milwauakee, WI

Anacostia Museum- Washington, DC

Anne Spencer House and Garden Museum-Lynchburg, VA

APEX (African American Panoramic Experience) Museum-Atlanta, GA

Arthur "Smokestack" Hardy Fire Museum- Baltimore, MD

Banneker-Douglass Museum-Annapolis MD

Benjamin Banneker Historical Park and Museum-Oella, MD

Bertha Lee Strickland Cultural Museum- Seneca, SC

Birmingham Civil Rights Institute- Birmingham, AL

Black American West Museum & Heritage Center- Denver, CO

Black Cowboy Museum-Rosenburg, TX

Black History 101 Mobile Museum-Detroit , MI

Black History Museum and Cultural Center of Virginia-Richmond VA

Bontemps African American Museum- Alexandria, LA

Brazos Valley African American Museum-Bryan Texas

Buffalo Soldiers National MuseumBuffalo Soldiers National Museum-Houston Texas

California African American Museum- Los Angeles, CA

Charles H. Wright Museum of African American History-Detroit, MI

Clemson Area African American Museum-Clemson, SC

Delta Cultural Center- Helena, Arkansas

Destination Crenshaw- Los Angeles, CA

Dorchester Academy and Museum- Midway, GA

Dr. Carter G. Woodson African American History Museum- St.Petersburg, Florida

DuSable Museum of African American History - Chicago, Illinois

Finding Our Roots African American Museum- Houma, LA

Frederick Douglass National Historic Site-Washington, D.C.

George Washington Carver Museum- Tuskegee, AL

George Washington Carver Museum- Phoenix, AZ

George Washington Carver Museum and Cultural Center - Austin, TX

Great Blacks in Wax Museum - Baltimore, MD

Great Plains Black History Museum- Omaha , NE

Griot Museum of Black History - St Louis, MO

Hammonds House Museum- Atlanta, GA

Harriet Tubman Underground Railroad Visitor Center- Church Creek,MD

Harvey B. Gantt Center - Charlotte,NC

Idaho Black History Museum- Boise, ID

International African American Museum-Charleston, SC

International Civil Rights Center and Museum- Greensboro, NC

John E. Rogers African American Cultural Center - Hartford, CT

John G. Riley Center/Museum of African American History and Culture - Tallahassee, FL

Kansas African-American Museum - Wichita , KS

L.E. Coleman African-American Museum - Halifax, VA

LaVilla Museum - Jacksonville , FL

The Legacy Museum- - Montgomery, AL

Legacy Museum of African American History - Lynchburg, VA

Lewis H. Latimer House - Queens, NY

Louis Armstrong House - - Queens NY

Martin Luther King, Jr., National Historic Site Visitors Center - Atlanta, GA

Mary McLeod Bethune Council House National Historic Site - Washington, DC

Mary McLeod Bethune Home - Daytona Beach, FL

Mary S. Harrell Black Heritage Museum - New Smyrna Beach, FL

Mayme A. Clayton Library and Museum - Culver City, CA

Mississippi Civil Rights Museum - Jackson, MS

MoCADA - Brooklyn , NY

Mosaic Templars Cultural Center - Little Rock, AK

Muhammad Ali Center- Louisville,KY

Museum of African American History & Abiel Smith School- Boston, MA

Museum of the African Diaspora- San Francisco, CA

Natchez Museum of African American History and Culture - Natchez, MS

National African American Archives and Museum - Mobile, AL

National Afro-American Museum and Cultural Center- Wilberforce,OH

National Center for Civil and Human Rights - Atlanta, GA

National Center of Afro- American Artists- Roxbury, MA

National Civil Rights Museum- Memphis, TN

National Museum of African American History and Culture- Washington, DC

National Museum of African American Music- Nashville, TN

National Underground Railroad Freedom Center - Nashville, TN

National Voting Rights Museum- Selma, AL

Negro Leagues Baseball Museum - Kansas City,MO

New Orleans African American Museum - New Orleans, LA

Niagara Falls Underground Railroad Heritage Center - Niagra Falls, NY

Northeast Louisiana Delta African American Heritage Museum - Monroe, LA

Northwest African American Museum -Seattle , WA

Odell S. Williams Now And Then African-American Museum- Baton Rouge, LA

Old Dillard Museum- Fort Lauderdale, FL

Oran Z's Black Facts and Wax Museum - Los Angeles, CA

Paul R. Jones Collection of African American Art - Newark, DE

Prince George's African American Museum and Cultural Center - North Brentwood, MD

Reginald F. Lewis Museum of Maryland African American History & Culture - Baltimore, MD

River Road African American Museum - Donaldsonville , LA

Rosa Parks Museum- Montgomery, AL

Rural African American Museum - Opelousas, LA

Sandy Ground Historical Museum- New York, NY

Slave Mart Museum - Charleston , SC

Smith-Robertson Museum and Cultural Center - Jackson, MS

Southeastern Regional Black Archives Research Center and Museum - Tallahassee , FL

Springfield and Central Illinois African-American History Museum- Springfield, IL

Studio Museum in Harlem- Harlem, NY

Tangipahoa African American Heritage Museum-Hammond, LA

Tubman African American
Museum - Macon , GA
Tuskegee Airmen National
Historic Site - Tuskegee, AL
Tuskegee Airmen National
Museum - Detroit, MI
Weeksville Heritage Center -
Brooklyn, NY
Wells' Built Museum - Orlando,
FL
Whitney Plantation - St.John
Parish, LA
Willam V. Banks Broadcast
Museum - Detroit,MI

Pilots Association-

Black Pilots of America
https://bpapilots.org/

International Black Aerospace
Council
http://www.blackaerospace.com/

Organization of Black Aerospace
Professionals
https://www.obap.org/

Ski Clubs

National Brotherhood of Skiers
Black Ski Summit
http://www.nbs.org/
Eastern Region

Eastern Region

Black Ski, Inc.Washington, DC

Blazers Ski ClubPhiladelphia, PA

Boston Ski PartyBoston, MA

Charlotte Breezers Ski & Sports
Club,
Inc.Charlotte, NC

Double DiamondsHartford, CT

Ice Breakers Ski ClubValley
Stream, NY
Jersey Ski & Sports, Inc.Newark,
NJ
Miami International Athletic Ski &
Sports Club, Inc.Miami, FL
Nubian Empire Ski Club Albany,
NY
Onyx Ski & Sports Club of
Tampa Bay Tampa/St.
Petersburg,FL
Sno-Burners Ski & SportsNew
York, NY
Snow Rovers-Boston (inactive)
Boston, MA

Soulboarders, Inc. New York, NY

Southern Snow Seekers Atlanta
GA
Steel On Ice Ski Club Pittsburgh,
PA

Sugar & Spice Snow & Social
Club Ft. Washington, MD
Sunshine Slopers Miami
Gardens, FL
The Sandblaster Skiers, Inc.
Atlantic City, NJ

Thrillseekers, Inc.Hollis, NY

Triad Diamond Ski ClubWinston-
Salem, NC

Midwest Region

Avalanche Ski Club
Montgomery, AL
Central Ohio Alpine Ski
TroopColumbus, OH

Chicago Ski Twisters Chicago, IL

Corbeau Ski Club Cincinnati, OH

Diamond Ice Ski Club
Kalamazoo, MI
Ebony Ice Ski Club Milwaukee,
WI
Esprit The Ultimate Ski & Sports
Club Cleveland OH
Gem City Gliders, Inc. Dayton,
OH
Inner City Ski Club, Inc.Bedford
Hts., OH
Jazz-Ma-Tazz Ski Club New
Orleans, LA
Jim Dandy Ski Club, Inc. Detroit
MI

PathfindersPeoria, IL

Show-Me-Skiers Ski Club St.
Louis, MO
Sno-Gophers Ski Club Chicago,
IL

Tenn-A-Ski Mavericks Memphis, TN

Umoja Ski Club Saginaw, MI

Rocky Mountain Region

Midwest Ski Kansas City Kansas City, KS

Ski Ambassadors of Colorado Springs Colorado Springs, CO

Ski Jammers Ski Club Houston, TX

Ski Noir 5280 Denver, CO

Slippers-N-Sliders Ski Club Denver, CO

Texas Ski Rangers Dallas, TX

Western Region

All Seasons Ski Club Oakland, CA

Blade Runners Ski Club Los Angeles, CA

Camellia City Ski ClubN. Highlands, CA

Ebony Ski & Racquet Club W. Sacramento, CA

Executive Board Snowboard Association Los Angeles, CA

Fire & Ice Ski Club San Jose, CA

Four Seasons West Ski & Snowboard Club Los Angeles, CA

Inland Empire Ski & Sports Riverside, CA

Mountain View Ski Club San Diego, CA

Sierra Snow Gliders, Inc.Las Vegas, NV

SnowBusters Ski Club Pasadena, CA

U2 Can Ski Club Stockton, CA

Winter Fox Ski Association Los Angeles, CA

International

Nubia Ski Club- London, England

Tourism Boardswith Black C level Executives-

2. Arthur Ayres, Jr.VP of Finance, Discover Philadelphia
3. Cleo BattleCOO, Louisville Tourism
4. Timothy BushPresident and CEO, Louisiana's Cajun Bayou
5. Julie CokerPresident and CEO, San Diego Tourism Authority
6. Gregory DeShields PHL Diversity, Executive Director, Discover Philadelphia
7. Jason Dunn Group VP, Diversity Sales & Inclusion, Cincinnati USA CVB
8. Lorne Edwards SVP of Sales and Services, Visit Phoenix
9. Elliott Ferguson President and CEO, Destination DC
10. Darren GreenSVP, Sales, LA Tourism & Convention Board
11. Michael Gunn SVP, Convention Sales and Servicing, Greater Birmingham CVB
12. Al HutchinsonPresident and CEO, Visit Baltimore
13. Charles Jeffers IICOO, Visit Baltimore
14. James JessieSVP of Convention Sales & Services, Travel Portland
15. Connie KinnardVP, Multicultural Tourism & Development Greater Miami CVB
16. Robin McClainSVP, Marketing and Communications, Destination DC
17. Angela NelsonVP of Multicultural Business Development, Experience Grand Rapids
18. Marie SueingVP, Multi-Cultural Community Relations, Nashville Convention & Visitors Corp
19. Melvin Tennant President & CEO, Meet Minneapolis
20. Rickey Thigpen President & CEO, Visit Jackson
21. Dan Williams VP, Convention Sales & Services, Experience Columbus
22. Ernest Wooden, Jr.President and CEO, LA Tourism & Convention Board

Yacht Clubs

Black Chicago Sailors
http://blackchicagosailors.org/

Seafarers Yacht Club
www.seafarersyc.com

Universal Sailing Company
https://universalsailingclub.org/

CONTINENTS/ COUNTRIES

Asia

The Black business app for Asia is BEJ Direct

Azerbaijan,

The Union of Africans in Azerbaijan- facebook group .
Most Africans live in Baku

Bahrain

Africans traditionally live in Muharraq Island, Riffa and study in Dhaka
Facebook group
African social Club in Bahrain

Beauty/ Cosmetics

Uncommon Human Hair Extensions Bahrain, +973 6666 0322

Restaurant

Kienyeji Lounge
Kikwetu Shop
Kingsboulevard

The African Pot
Bahrain Manama road 521 00973
Manama, Bahrain

Tours

Bahrain Safari

Bangladesh,

Community

Chittagong- Increasing African community
Dhaka has a community of Africans, studying

Cambodia

Restaurants

African Otres Bar & Kitchen, Preah Sihanouk, Cambodia, +855 97 320 0769

Oma Foods,
T147 Street Norodom Cominue HW4H+G7 Phnom Penh Phnom Penh, 20014, Cambodia, +855 97 390 0304

Onwa Foods, Street 18, Street 28B, 12351, Cambodia +855 97 390 0304

Sara Ethiopian Restaurant and Coffee Shop, #Eo1, Jayavarman 7 St. (172), Phnom Penh, Cambodia, +855 70 363 041

China

Community

Africa Week- last week in July
Brothas&Sistas of China-FB group
Black Life China-FB group

Beijing

Community
Black expo - Held in March

Restaurant

Kilimanjaro African Bar,
138 Jiaodaokou Nandajie,
Dongcheng District,
东城区

Pili Pili,
9-6 Jiangtai West Road (across
from the Rosedale Hotel),
Chaoyang District

Ras Ethipoian Food,
7 Sanlitun Lu,
Beijing, China,
86 10 6468 6053

Turays African restaurant,
Add: 2F, Unit 5, International
Wonderland,
39 Xingfu Ercun, Chaoyang
District, Beijing,
地址: 北京市朝阳区幸福二村39号
首开广场5号单元2层,
Tel: 010 8444 4169
交道口南大街138号,
Daily 2pm-1am, 8404 2298

Shanghai

Restaurants

Kaiba
528 Kangding Lu
Near Xikang Lu

Salons/Barbershop

Crown Salon

The ABC Travel Greenbook

9/F, 831 Xinzha Lu, near Shimen
Er Lu
HAIR Online
1033 Kangding Lu,
near Yanping Lu
康定路1033号, 近延平路

Paulma Salon
2/F, 229 Zhejiang Zhong Lu,
near Hankou Lu
浙江中路229号2楼, 近汉口路

STECY BENZ 's WiGs
+86 131 9786 8201

Hong Kong

Nathan Road is the black
community

Restaurants

Kaiba
528 Kangding Lu
Near Xikang Lu

Kwality
Chungking Mansions, 36-44
Nathan Road
Tsim Sha Tsui, Hong Kong

Makumba
2/F, Ho Lee Commercial
Building, 38-44 D'Aguilar Street,
Lan Kwai Fong, Central

Zanziba
29B 1st Floor, Mirador Mansion,
58 Nathan Road
Tsim Sha Tsui

Hong Kong

Salons/Barbershops

Braiding shops
Mirador Mansion, 54 - 58 Nathan
rd, 1 floor , Shop 18, near to TST
MTR station exit D2, Tsim Sha
Tsui, Hong Kong

Sista Precious. (African/Black
American/Afro Braids in Hong
kong)

Taiwan

Brothas & Sistas of Taiwan FB
group

Taipei

Restaurants

Samba's place
No.8, Lane 8, Wuxing Street
吳興街8巷8號

Xinyi District, 台北市 106

Taichung

Restaurants

ALTA Nightclub
西屯區青海南街59號1至2樓
Taichung, Taiwan 407
+886 922 536 688
Arts and Crafts-Bar
台中市西屯區西屯路三段166-87
號一樓 Taichung, Taiwan 407
+886 4 2461 1227

Guangzhou-Largest African
community in Asia
Shelby Road is where all African
businesses are.

Nanjing

Restaurant

Chaley
No.136 Shandong Road,
Xinjiekou | No.136-5, Zhongshan
east road, Nanjing, China +86
156 5172 5575

Georgia- Afro Georgians are
referred to as Afro-Abkhazians.
They can be found in the two
regions of Adzyubzha and
Kodori Gorge

Indonesia,

Ubud

Black in Bali Community-FB
Black in Bali- FB

Entertainment

Black Bali Fest

Restaurants

Jambali Jamaican Restaurant -
Michelle
Jl. Penestanan Kelod, Ubud
85071, Indonesia

Iran- Afro-Iranian

Iraq- Afro Iraqi
Black people are in the southern city of Basra- 2 million

Israel

This region has a black population of Ethiopian Jews. I chose to focus on the thriving community where you can support black businesses when traveling there.

Elliat

Restaurant

Fast Habesha Restaraunt
Sderot HaTmarim 37, Eilat, Israel
+972 8-853-5193

Haifa

Restaurants

Mothers
20 Ha-Nevi'im Within a building complex courtyard, Haifa 3330504 Israel

Herzliya

מסעדה אתיופית
Ben Gurion Blvd 15, Herzliya, Israel
+972 77-404-7200

Jerusalem

Restaurants

El Shadday Ethiopian Restaurant
9, HaHavatselet St 5, Jerusalem, Israel
+972 54-788-8136

Havash Bar And Restaurant
Mashiyah Barukhof St 3, Jerusalem, Israel
+972 54-876-8528

Shegar Ethiopian Restaurant
Agripas St 20, Jerusalem, Israel
+972 55-666-4379

Sheba Ethiopian Restaurant
10, Ya'avets St 2, Jerusalem, Israel
+972 52-249-1181
Queen of Sheba Restaurant
Ya'avets St 2, Jerusalem, Israel
+972 54-727-4413

Walia Ibex
Jaffa St 28, Jerusalem, Israel
+972 2-355-4500

מסעדה אתיופית
Havatselet St 3, Jerusalem, Israel
+972 2-585-1394

Salons/Barbershops

Hair Braiding
Find Ethiopian braiding salons on Agrippas street Street in the section between Machane Yehuda market and Ben Zvi Boulevard.

Kiryat Ata

Community

Netanya- largest Ethiopian community in Israel
Neighborhood - Shikun Vatikim

Restaurants

Old shopping area, north-west corner of main intersection, Kiryat Ata,
+972 50-459-9989

Tel Aviv

Neighborhood- Beit Ambousa, Gedera , Neve Sha'anan
בייא-Bayanto
Goldenhirsh St 2, Petah Tikva, Israel
+972 50-424-5813

Restaurants

Ahtnt Bar
Rehov Agripas 78, Jerusalem 2423625 Israel
+972 50-213-8833

Balinjera
Rehov Malan 4, Tel Aviv Israel
+972 3-525-2527
Ethiopia Restaurant
13 Allenby, Tel Aviv Israel
+972 52-351-5929

Habesh
Mashiyah Barukhof St 5, Jerusalem 9662221 Israel

Lalibela
43 Ha-Aliya, Tel Aviv

6604116 Israel

Lucy Ethiopian Restaurant
Derech Menachem Begin 48,

Tel Aviv Israel

Maganda
Rehov Rabbi Meir 26, Tel Aviv Israel
+972 3-517-9990

Tenat
Chelnov 27, Tel Aviv 6604809 Israel
+972 3-522-2829

Tenat
Rehov Chlenov 27, Tel Aviv Israel
+972 3-522-2829

Theodros Ethiopian Restaurant
Tel Aviv Israel
+972 57-942-6807

Walia Ibex
Rehov Jaffa 28, Jerusalem Israel
+972 2-355-4500

Salons/Barbershops

BalbalaRasta
יואל משה סלומון 21 9463319 Jerusalem, Israel
+972 77-535-4655

Kundala Rasta Hair braiding and dreadlocks

44 King George St, near
Dizengoff Center. Tel 03-620-
7045.

Tours

Tel Aviv Discovery Tour: Meet
the Ethiopian Community of
Israel

Rehovot

Restaurants

Gojo Restaurant
Israel Teller St 32, Rehovot,
Israel
+972 8-996-4644

Japan

Community

Tokyo Black professionals
Africa in Japan
Black experience japan

Entertainment

Ibex NightClub

Fitness

PatFit
2F Seiko Bldg, 27-1
Sakuragaokacho, Shibuya,
Tokyo 〒150-0031

Restaurants

Addis Mediterranean
2 Chome-3-15 Nakane, Meguro-
ku, Tōkyō-to 152-0031

03-6421-4302

Africa Tairiku
吉祥寺南町2-13-4..オフィスワン
地下103
Musashino, 東京都 〒180-0003
Japan Kichijojiminamicho,
Kichijoji Station,
Inokashira-koen Station

Bistro New Orleans
Address: ＣＯＬＬＥＴ北堀江 1-
15, 1
Chome-10-13 Kitahorie, Nishi
Ward, Osaka,
550-0014, Japan
Phone: +81 6-6543-7071

Cafe Orleans
Address: 2 Chome-33-16
Futenma, Ginowan, Okinawa
901-2202, Japan
Phone: +81 98-892-
8677..Sirena..2-chōme-13
.Shinjuku..Shinjuku City, Tōkyō-
to 160-0022

Calabash
浜松町2丁目10-1
浜松町ビルＢ１Ｆ
Minato, 東京都 〒105-0013
Japan

Dalia
日本橋大伝馬町2-9
Chūō, 東京都 〒103-0012
Japan

Didi Grande

Continents/Countries

2 Chome-16-10 Azabujuban
Murata Bldg 1F Minato City,
Tokyo, 106-0045
+81 3-6275-1550

Eko Loyloyon
赤坂2-17-72..イーデンビル2F
Minato, 東京都 〒107-0052
Japan Akasaka Station
 +81 3 6277 6979
Esogie
新宿3-11-2
村木ビル 3F
Shinjuku, 東京都 〒160-0022
Japan

Shinjyuku-Sanchome Station,
Shinjuku Station, Shinjuku
Gyoen Mae Station
+81 3 3353 3334
Hamamatsucho Station.

Kyle's Good Finds
2-7-10 Arai Nakano-ku Tokyo 13
165-0026 jp
L'azure
百人町1-24-8..新宿タウンプラザ
ビル 2F
Shinjuku, 東京都 〒169-0073
Japan

Okubo Station, Seibu Shinjuku
Station, Shinokubo Station
+81 3 3366 4004

Les Amis D'ami
渋谷区恵比寿2丁目87
Shibuya, 東京都 〒150-0013
Japan
81 3 3441 0633

Oncle Yves
桜台3-14-13..Nerima, 東京都 〒
176-0002
Japan..Hikawadai Station
+81 90 9803 4765

Padi's Tokyo
六本木3-13-10..Koda Building 5F
Minato, 東京都 〒106-0032
Japan..Roppongi Station
+81 3 6698 9001

Queen Sheba
1 Chome-3-1 Higashiyama,
Meguro City, Tokyo 153-0043,
Japan
TEL/FAX: 03-3794-1801

Safari House
赤坂3-13-1
ベルズ赤坂　2Ｆ
Minato, 東京都 〒107-0052
Japan
Akasaka Station,
Akasakamitsuke Station

Savanna
経堂1-19-7
セントラル経堂 B1F
Setagaya, 東京都
Japan
Kyodo Station
+81 3 3428 4040

Soul Food house
2-8-10 6F Patio AZABUJUBAN,
Azabujuban, Minato 106-0045
Tokyo Prefecture
+81 3-5765-2148

Tam Tamu
松庵3-18-15
Suginami, 東京都 〒167-0054
Japan
Nishi-ogikubo Station, Kichijoji
Station
+81 3 6320 9937

Yinega.
東京都渋谷区渋谷1-10-2
志水ビル1階
Shibuya, 東京都 Japan
Shibuya Station Miya Masuzaka-
guchi, Shibuya Station
Phone number
+81 90 8507 8728

Salons/Barbershops

Black hair salon japan
shinjuku-ku nishi shinjuku 7-1-7
daikan plaza A 301 Shinjuku
160-0023
+81 3-3371-4777

Hair Dresser Tokyo
shinjuku-ku nishi shinjuku 7-1-7
Daikan plaza A 301 Shinjuku
160-0023
+81 3-3371-4777

Hair salon for braids in tokyo
nishi shinjuku 7-1-7 daikan plaza
A 301
Shinjuku 160-0023
+81 3-3371-4777

Oriental Magic
Stylist: Aya
098-926-4545

Okinawa, Japan
Submitted Sunday, October 11,
2015 at 10:11

Professional Braids Extension
03-3371-4777
Shinjuku-ku nishi shinjuku 7-1-7
Daikan plaza A-301
tokyo, Japan

Room 806
5 chome-16-52 Roppongi,
Minato City, Tokyo 106-0032
+81 3-5545-5486

Shop Brooklyn
6 chome 23-13 2A Jingumae,
Shibuya City, Tokyo 150-0001
+818043220462

Jordan

Al-Ghor (the Jordan River
Valley)
Afro-Palestinian community

Kuwait

Brothas and Sistas of Kuwait-FB

Restaurants

Reggae Vybz Kitchen

Salons/Barbershops

Black Owned Hair Salon in
Mangaf now open. This is for
ladies only. Block 1, Firestation
St. Buidling 5, 2nd Floor.

Teddy-barber-96566593817

Mohammed-barber-
96550303582

Transportation

Global Opportunities General
Trading and Contracting
Cathy
+96599083248

Oman

Entertainment

https://www.facebook.com/africo
m.oman

Africa Day Festival- June

Grocery and Convenience Stores

African groceries oman - +968
9558 5463
Marbella near nestor hypermaket
Opposite platinum hotel Muscat
OM, 112, Oman
J4QR+C7 Seeb, Oman

Pakistan

Has the largest descent of
Africans in South Asia- Called
the Sheedi
Can be found in Sindh and
Balochistan
Sheedi-Mela is the annual
African Festival

Advocacy group:Sheedi Youth
Welfare

Philippines- Aeta Negritos

Qatar

Brothas and Sistas of Qatar

Singapore

Church

Cornerstone African House of
Praise

Entertainment

Africa Parties Singapore

Black Net Singapore-
https://blacknetsg.com/

Mama Africa Singapore

Restaurant

Kafe Utu +65 6996 3937
https://www.kafeutu.com/

South Korea

Beauty/ Cosmetics

Camp Beauty Supply..+82 10-
5232-5657..Camp Humphreys

Honey Hair Beauty Supply..+82
31-655-5307..222 Beongil
Building 106, Paengseong-eup

Anjeongri, Pyeongtaek, Gyeonggi-do 17982 Pyeongtaek 17982

Itaewon Beauty Supply..+82 10-9983-3272..http://www.itwbeauty.com/

Entertainment

Seoul Africa Fashion Week..https://www.seoulafricafashionshow.com/

Restaurant

Casa Blanca Sandwicherie @casablancasandwicherie +82 2-797-8367 Yongsan-gu, Yongsan-dong 2ga 44-7 Seoul, Korea 140-842

Happy Home Restaurant @happyhomerestaurant +82 2-797-3185 2F,64-15 Itaewon-dong,Youngsan-gu. Seoul, Korea 140-863

Island Bites +82 31-666-1336 경기도 Pyeongtaek 중앙시장로 19번길 10

Itaewon

Restaurants

Braai Republic

@braairepublic 82 70-8879-1967 http://www.braairepublic.com/ Itaewon-ro 14-gil, Itaewon 1(il)-dong, Yongsan-gu, Seoul, South Korea

JJ's Diner +82 31-8094-1337 113-88 Angeongri, Pyeongtaek, Gyeonggi-do 17983 Pyeongtaek 179-83

Jollof Africa Korea..@Jollof_Africa_korea

Pie republic Korea..@pierepublickorea..+82 2-6083-1967..서울특별시 마포구 양화로23길 10-10, 지하1층 B102호(동교동) Seoul, Korea 03985

Snack Shack Korea..@snackshackkorea..+82 10-2898-2360..49 Jungang-daero, Jungang-dong Changwon

Salons/Barbershops

Angels Hair Braiding..seoul yongsan gu Itaewon dong Seoul, Korea 118-34..+82 10-3064-7167

Nelly Hair Braiding Itaewon..+82 10-7219-4421

Precious Hair Braids Osan

@precious_hair_braids_osan
+82 10-7652-8111..Opposite
Osan Main gate
Gyeonggi'do
South korea Osan, Kyonggi-Do,
Korea 17758

Terry Hair Braid
CAMP WALKER GATE 4 Daegu
705-023.
+82 10-2134-9599

Sri Lanka

Afro Sri Lankan's were brought
to the country in the 1700's .
Also know as Kaffirs
They can be found in
Trincomalee, Batticaloa
Negombo.

Syria

Afro Syrians can be found by
Yarmouk Basin River

Thailand

Brothas and sistas of Thailand-
FB
Brothas and sistas of Chiang
Mai-FB

Restaurants

Fidel Ethiopian

Jamaican Eatz
Pridi Banomyong 3 Alley, Phra
Khanong Nuea, Khlong Toei,
Bangkok 10110 Bangkok,
Thailand 10110

+66 95 945 9738

Salons/ Barbershops

Noi salon (black and beauty
shop) 122/60 soi somprasong
Rajprarop RD, Prautnam ,
Bangkok. (092-7340924) .The
small shop belongs to a Thai
woman and she has African hair
stylists.
Phuket-

Timor-Leste (East Timor),

African community in Timor-
Leste FB

Turkey

Afro Turks are small in number
and can be found throughout
Turkey. To celebrate their
African routes They have their
annual festival Dana Bayram.

Restaurants

Askasary Market has african
food
Website for everyone as in most
braiding spots is
Nijeryalikuafor.com

Location Of Habesha Restaurant
Hüseyin Ağa Mh. Ekrem Tur Sk.
No:5 Beyoğlu/İST
Contact: +905322677066

Salons/Barbershops

Royal Mark Saloon
Sisli Bozkurt Ergenekon Caddesi
Muratogulucarsin Pangalti
No.41 B13

CAKIRAGA .MAH.KATIP
MUSLHIDDIN SK.NO.30-B
AKSARAY-ISTANBUL
Istanbul, Turkey 34096
Get Directions
+90 534 377 54 93

Chichi African Hair Braiding
@chichi_africa_hair_braiding

United Arab Emirates

Dubai + Abu Dhabi
Brothas and Sistas of Dubai-FB

Entertainment

Black photog
https://www.instagram.com/reidt
weendaline/
https://www.instagram.com/afros
abroad/

Black photog dessert shoot

Party In Dubai every friday -
Afrocentric

@iamafrocentric

Restaurants

Boon Coffee

Cluster T‹ Lake Plaza - Shop no.
21, Ground
Floor - Dubai - United Arab
Emirates

Catfish
Silver Tower , Marasi Dr ,
Business Bay
Dubai - United Arab Emirates

Kiza
Ground floor, ,Emirates Financial
Towers,Sheikh Zayed
Road,DIFC
Dubai - United Arab Emirates

Oh Brgr- Carribean Burger Joint
Cluster R, MAG 214 Tower -
Dubai - United Arab Emirates
https://www.instagram.com/ohbr
gr/

Dubai Speciality Coffee Tour-
Airbnbn
https://www.airbnb.com/experien
ces/732617
The Gbemi's Kitchen
Al Waleed Paradise, Shop 3,
Cluster R
Dubai - United Arab Emirates

West to West Kitchen – Abu
Dhabi
Al Bzaymi St - Zone 1E11
Abu Dhabi - United Arab

Salons/Barbershops

Afro Beauty Salon -
https://www.afrobeauty.ae/

Shop 48, al Attar Business
Centre Ground
Floor Sheikh Zayed Road, al
Barsha 1, Dubai

Braids Ladies Salon
Muroor Rd - Zone 1E20-02
Abu Dhabi - United Arab
Emirates

Fade and Play Barbershop
Trio Building, Shop 20
Dubai - United Arab Emirates

Wellness

Afro Fit -Dubai

Uzbekistan- Black people aren't
seen in this region often. You will
get stares. Travel aware and on
alert.

Vietnam

There are black people in
vietnam partially due to the
soldiers who were there and had
kids. There also is a community
of black expats . Soul Alley is
black history in vietname. It was
a street created for the black
soldiers back during the war.

Events

The Black Excellence Showcase
and Festival - July Saigon

Saigon.

Blacks in Hanoi-FB group
Hanoi: The Black Experience-FB
group

Beauty/ Cosmetics

HCMC Black star beauty supply
+84 33 420 4454
Nicole and Brian

Entertainment

The Venue
46 An Duong
Hanoi, Vietnam
Get Directions
+84 33 359 5915

Restaurants

Escape
Jamaica Jamaica -closed
Out of africa Nanoi -Ngo 41 Tay
Ho street , Tay Ho, Ha Noi,
Vietnam

Salons/Barbershops

Barber - Young and Nice
Call +84 39 869 5480
m.me/youngandnicetv
donkorjsn@gmail.com

Wunmi Hair products
Wunmihair.com
107 Au co Hanoi, Vietnam 10000

Grace Afro Beauty Hair
89/189 Hoàng Hoa Thám, Ngọc
Hồ, Ba Đình, Hà Nội Hanoi,
Vietnam 100100
+84 83 809 4329

Lady s Afro salon
Vietnam Hanoi, Vietnam 0311

QueenDee Afro Hair salon
5c 236 / 11 Au Co.Tay Ho.
Hanoi Hanoi, Vietnam 10000

Yemen- There is a Afro-Yemen community known as the Ahkdam or the Muhamasheen. They are treated poorly by the government and are seen as less than.

Australia

For a full list of black owned businesses including fashion and professional services please visit buy-black-owned.com/

Facebook communities

Sistas in Australia & New Zealand
Black Owned Sydney
Black Owned Regional NSW
Black Owned Western Australia
Black Owned Northern Territory
Black Owned South Australia
Black Owned Tasmania (original)
Black Owned Australian Capital Territory
Black Owned Brisbane
Black Owned Melbourne

Jamaican Association of Australia
http://jaaustralia.org.au/

Beauty/ Cosmetics

Xceptional makeup and beauty products
www.xceptionalmakeup.com

Entertainment

Africa Day Australia -
http://www.africadayaustralia.org/ - 25th of MAY

Sounds of Africa Festival -
http://soafestival.com.au/ -
https://www.facebook.com/soafest

Restaurants

African Food Australia
https://www.africanfind.com/

Salons/Barbershops

Lizz dee hair braiding

Brisbane

Entertainment

Let's Gather Events & Catering
Unit 406 White Ibis Drive Griffin
0415 541985 or 0423 280 451
https://letsgather.wixsite.com/australia

Canberra

Entertainment

Canberra Afro All White Party-December

Salons/Barbershops

Afro-cuts
+61 426 195 523
ikamara45@hotmail.com

Rachsy Hair & Beauty salon Canberra
3Harold Blair crescent moncrieff Act Canberra,
ACT, Australia 2914

Melbourne

Bakery/ Sweets

Sweets by Semi

Facebook community
Nigerians in Melbourne

Entertainment

African Music Festival -
November
Footscray is the black
neighborhood
Melbourne Splash Festival -
February,
@melbourne_splash_festival

Restaurants

Ge'ez Ethiopian,
718 Sydney Rd. Brunswick ,
Melbourne 8354 0124

Kitchen After Dark,
http://kitchenafterdark.com.au/

Tasty Suya African Bbq-Caterer
and Markets,
@tastysuyaafricabbq,
tastysuyaabbq@yahoo.com
+61 469 394 744

Salons/Barber Shops

Cynthia's African Hair Braids,
51 Main Rd W Melbourne,
VIC, Australia 3021

The perfect Barber Shop
Melbourne
207 Johnston St, Collingwood

VIC 3066, Australia

Wellness

Baby Sitting by Tee,
taidachiggs@gmail.com

Miliner Darwin

Salons/Barber Shops

African Beauty Salon
Shop 3/2 Sabine Road, Millner
Darwin, NT,
Australia 0810

Glamour Touch African Hair
Braiding Darwin,
https://www.braidingdarwin.com.
au/services
+61 402 929 774

Look Fabulous,
+61 422 775 569

Northwest Territory

Salons/Barbershops

Jabarii Hair&Beauty Salon,
Alice Springs, NT, Australia
0870,
+61 484 936 668

Perth

Beauty/ Cosmetics

Jimani beauty,
Hammond Park WA 6164,
Australia

Entertainment

Continents/Countries

Perfect Promotions,
@perfectpromotions

Salons/Barbershops

Lib-bab hair extensions,
36 worthington road Elizabeth
 East Adelaide, SA,
Australia 5112

The perfect barber,
4/17 Green street .
Mount Hawthorn, Perth

Sydney

Beauty/ Cosmetics

Rumbie & Co.,
14/128 Cleveland St
Chippendale,
NSW, Australia 2008,
http://www.rumbie.co/
+61 2 9318 0698,
https://www.facebook.com/theoffi
cialrumbie

Community Groups

August Inc.,
https://www.august-inc.com/,
https://www.facebook.com/augus
tincaus

Entertainment

Ceremonies By Karen Posener,
https://www.ceremoniesbykaren
posener.com/

Wedding Celebrant

Restaurants

Charcoal Kitchen- order online,
thecharcoalkitchensydney@gmai
l.com
 +61 421 344 090

Jamaican Delight,
info@jamaicandelight.com.au
 Northern Beaches African
Foods,
+61 424 990 233

The Baza Queenskitchen

Salons/Barbershops

Curls and Natural Hair,
https://www.curlsandnaturalhair.
com.au/ ,
Shop1, 1271 Botany Road,
Mascot, NSW 2020,
+61 432 763 555,
info@curlsandnaturalhair.com.au

The Braid Bar - Mobile braiding
(for parties and events),
http://www.thebraidboss.com/,
+61 449 022 559,

New South Wales - Sydney

Accommodation

The Village: Ikhaya lembali -
Glamping grounds
Wollongong, NSW, Australia
2529,
+61 420 449 769,
ikhayalembali@gmail.com

Bakery/ Sweets

African bites
https://www.africanbites.com.au/

Sarah's Cupcaake Creations,
Blacktown, NSW, Australia 2148

Beauty/ Cosmetics

G&T Beauty,
Suite 8, 2 Bungan Lane, Mona
Vale NSW,
+61 432 116 879
@gandtbeauty_monavale

Fitness

Afro Step Sydney
@afrostepsydney

Sheron Fits Sultan
https://sheronfitsultan.com.au/,
train@sheronfit.com/au, 0403
325 950

Restaurants

African Feeling Catering
Restaurants,
794 Parramatta rd Lewisham
@The Luis Hotel Lewisham
Sydney, NSW, Australia

EL- Shaddai African Cuisine,
350 Guildford Road, Sydney,
NSW, Australia 2160

Little Lagos,

125 Enmore Road Enmore,
NSW, Australia 2042

Salons/Barbershops

Afrocuts, Bankstown

NSW 2200, Australia

Alicia Cosmetics & Hair Braiding,
Shop 8/20 MC farlane street
Merrylands,
NSW, Australia 2160

Braids of Africa Hair Extensions,
Inner west Sydney NSW
Australia Sydney,
NSW, Australia 2133
Ladysee Beauty Salon-FB,
Yagoona, NSW, 61 450 956 261

Sista's Store,
Selling Afro Caribbean Hair &
Food .

Queensland - (Brisbane)

Church

RCCG House of Praise,
Caboolture,
1 Lee Street, Caboolture,
Queensland.
Brisbane, QLD, Australia 4510,
http://www.rccghopcaboolture.or
g.au/

Community
Central Queensland African
Association

43 sheehy street Rockhampton, QLD, Australia 4701

Restaurants

Cush sudanese, Mu'ooz, made in Africa

Salons/Barber Shops
Cairns Hair Braiding & Extensions,
Mills close, Manoora Cairns, QLD,
Australia 4870
Kani's Affordable Box Braiding Service,
+61 411 842 903

Mama Afrique Pty Ltd,
3/68 SYDNEY STREET Mackay, QLD,
Australia 4740

Memo Hair African Hairdressing,
20 Gregory St Mackay, QLD,
Australia 4740

MVP Cutz, 7/5 Smith road , Goodna, Queensland, Australia

Pettys Hair Braiding,
Koongal Rockhampton City, QLD, Australia 4701

Victoria

Beauty/ Cosmetics

Jimani beauty, Xceptional Makeup & Beauty,

Townsend Street Wyndham Vale, VIC,
Australia 3024,
http://www.xceptionalmakeup.com/,
+61 401 873 687

Community

The Black Collective "TBC"
https://www.facebook.com/TheBlackCollectiveAU

Entertainment

Miss Africa Victoria Australia Pageant,
https://www.facebook.com/missafricavictoriaaustralia

Restaurant

Adonai Foods,
478 Drummond Street Carlton, VIC, Australia 3053

Angies Kitchen -Ghanaian food,
itsangieskitchen@gmail.com,
+61 469 437 149

Salons/Barbershops

African Multicultural Hair and Beauty Salon
 bensonhurts parade Hoppers Crossing,
VIC,
Australia 3030

New Zealand

Auckland

Community

Black Creatives Aotearoa-FB

African Communities New
Zealand (within their group are
sub groups for those from
Ghana, Nigeria, Somalia, Kenya,
Uganda,Rwanda, Sudan,
Congolese, Burundi, Ethopian,
Oromo, Malawi, Zimbabwe)

https://acofi.org.nz/
acofi.akld@gmail.com

Auckland University African
Society

africansociety.uoa@gmail.com

University of Auckland Auckland,

New Zealand 1010

Entertainment
 African Film Festival New
Zealand,
 21 Millais St Grey Lynn
 Auckland, New Zealand 1245

http://www.africanfilmfestivalnz.o
rg.nz/,
+64 21 145 1337

Recreation

Yoga with Wendy Douglas,
5A, 2 Matakana Valley Road

The European Union-

In most cases, you will find black people throughout the most popular cities of Europe. In Eastern Europe you will get more stares as you might be one of the first black people they have ever seen. Be prepared to be stared at, or people being overly eager to meet you. In this section I will tell you country by country the racial climate.
Black Women in Europe™ - FB group to consider before traveling.

Albania

Albania is safe to travel to as a solo traveler, you will receive stares. There a re Afro Albanians throughout the country but they try to stay together.

Andorra

When traveling to this country please be aware of your surroundings. Black residents and tourist aren't always seen by natives so they will stare.

Armenia-

Armenians aren't use to seeing black people. They will stare and ask to take photos. If you are American they might be confused how you are American but your

skin isn't white. Please travel in Armenia alert and aware as usual.

Austria-

Afro Austrians are small in number but have been in this country since the 15th century. The majority of the black people you see came for education. You can find the majority of black people in Vienna. They have Organisations such as Pamoja: The Movement of the Young African Diaspora in Austria and the annual African Diaspora Youth Forum in Europe and Fresh Magazine, a publication on Black Austrian lifestyle, all color the lines of the nation's borders.

Community

Nigerian Igbo Union Upper Austria- FB Group
I REP NAIJA IN AUSTRIA(PROUD NIGERIANS) - FB Group

Graz

Restaurants

Omoka African Restaurant , Keplerstraße 12 8020 Graz, Austria

Vienna

Grocery

Lords exotic supermarket

Burggasse 113, 1070
Wien, Austria

Restaurants

Marvins Kitchen
 Hohlweggasse 15, 1030
Wien, Austria

Mama's African Grill
Steudelgasse 25, 1100
Wien, Austria

Cafe Lalibela
Schulgasse 7, 1180
Wien, Austria

African Restaurant Ikaze Verein
Lokal
Donau-City-Straße 1,
1220 Wien, Austria

Azerbaijan

There aren't a large amount of
Black residents or tourists who
visit. So when they do see Black
people they stare and might
even touch. Please be aware
and alert like you would be in
any other country

Community

The Union of Africans in
Azerbaijan

Belarus

There aren't a large amount of
Black residents or tourists who
visit. So when they do see Black
people they stare and look at

you as if you're "exotic" . The
majority of Black people who live
in Belarus are in MinskPlease be
aware and alert like you would
be in any other country

Belgium

Afro Belgians can be found
throughout the country with a
high number being from the
congo and Senegal.

Brussels

Black History Month is March
Brussels has the largest black
population in the country. The
predominantly Black
neighborhood is called Matongé
. This is where you'll find all the
black owned businesses. It's
next to the city center and easy
to get to through public
transportation.

Grocery

Baig Food
Rue Ropsy Chaudron 4,
1070 Brussels, Belgium

Bois d'Ebene Bruxelles Sprl
Boulevard du Midi 122,
1000 Bruxelles, Belgium

Restaurants

Café Béguin
Place du Samedi 12A,
1000 Bruxelles, Belgium
Cafebeguin.be
+32 2 217 76 22

Cap African
Rue Longue Vie
13 1050 Ixelles, Belgium

Cauribar
Chaussée d'Alsemberg
163 1190 Brussels, Belgium

Chez Faso du Niger
Rue Heyvaert 75,
1080 Anderlecht, Belgium

Chez Kirikou
Rue Longue Vie 20,
1050 Ixelles, Belgium

Jimmys Restaurant
http://www.jimmy-hoo.com/
+32 2 534 73 78

Le Kalu Ethnic Food
83 rue de l'église Saint-Gilles
1060 Brussel, Belgium
+32 486 61 98 44

Le New Makossa
Rue Longue Vie 18,
1050 Ixelles, Belgium

Le Nil
Boulevard Maurice Lemonnier
165,
1000 Bruxelles, Belgium

Le Pelisson
Rue Berckmans 26,
1060 Bruxelles, Belgium

Le Soho
Rue Longue Vie 17,
1050 Ixelles, Belgium

L'Horloge du Sud - Restaurant
Africain
Rue du Trône 141,
1050 Ixelles, Belgium

Horlogedusud.be

Kicoucou
Rue de la Crèche 17,
1050 Ixelles, Belgium

Ler Mboa Sprl
Rue de l'Argonne 28,
1060 Saint-Gilles, Belgium

Madagasikara
Rue de Flandre 10,
1000 Bruxelles, Belgium
+32 473 44 40 74

Mere Malou
Chaussee de Wavre,
1050 Brussels, Belgium

New Africana
Boulevard du Midi 110,
1000 Bruxelles, Belgium

Senegal
Chaussée de Wavre 114
1050 Ixelles, Belgium

Restaurant Congolais "Inzia"
Rue de la Paix 37,
1050 Ixelles, Belgium

Restaurant rwandais "La Boule
Bleue"
Chaussée de Wavre 115,
1050 Bruxelles, Belgium

Solel di Afrique
Soleil d'Afrique, Rue Longue Vie
10,
Brussels, Belgium,

Toukoul
Rue de Laeken 34,
1000 Bruxelles, Belgium
Toukoul.be

Salons/Barbershops

Akwaba
Rue de la Crèche 7,
1050 Ixelles, Belgium

Bamia
Chaussée de Wavre 30,
1050 Ixelles, Belgium

Global Air Concept
Rue Froissart 60,
1040 Etterbeek, Belgium

Nizoma
Chaussée de Wavre
30 1050 Ixelles, Belgium

We2Best
Chaussée de Wavre 21,
1050 Ixelles, Belgium

Tour

Brussels Black Heritage Tour

Wellness

Afro Yoga
http://www.afroyoga.be/

Kuumba - Flemish African House
Waverse steenweg 78
1050 Brussels

Bosnia and Herzegovina-

Black people don't live or travel to Bosnia often. There are less than 100 in the country, and because of it when they do see Black people they are intrigued. They will want to talk and take photos. If there are any they live in Sarajevo

Bulgaria

The Black people in Bulgaria are usually athletes or students. They are mainly in Sofia. It is not common to see a black person but you will be treated with respect.

Africans in Bulgaria- FB Group
NIGERIA-BULGARIA-FB Group
Africans Association and Sympathizers i n Bulgaria - FB Group

Croatia

Although not many black people here, you will find them in pockets of Zagreb, Zagorje and Samobor
.

Croatia Mega Yacht Experience 2021- Up In the Air Life . July and August

Cyprus

You will find a influx of Black students from Nigeria ,Cameroon and Zimbabwe in Cyprus, but they aren't always treated like they are welcome. They aren't always able to get jobs and they have trouble with the police. As a Black British or American, once they hear your accent you are treated differently.

Community

African Diaspora in Cyprus-FB group
Nigerian Community Cyprus-FB group
Nigerian Community Association Cyprus-FB group
Nigerians in Cyprus-FB group
Nigerian students in Cyprus-FB group

Famagusta

Restaurants

Elite Restaurant Afrika
Famagusta 99450
+90 533 848 83 00

Home African Restaurant
Eastern Mediterranean university,
Famagusta ,Las Gidi Restaurant

Gazi Mustafa Kemal Blv, Döveç
 Elite Life Building, Shop no
22 Famagusta/NORTH
Nicosa
Restaurants

African Gold
 Uluslararasi Kibris Universitesi Kampus,
+90 533 862 69 44

African Pot
Bayraktar Sk, Lefkoşa 99010
+90 533 873 03 53

Salons/Barbershops

Afro Dream Hair & Beauty

Rigenis 36, Nicosia, Cyprus
+357 97 680339

Czechia (Czech Republic)

There are droves of Black people in Prague and because it is such a cosmopolitan city now, it's not uncommon to see Black people. Please note there are skin heads in prague but they are more in the towns than the city. There have been no reports on racism but visit alert and aware as you would anywhere else

Community

Africans in Czech Republic-FB group
Africans in Czech-FB group
Skilled Africans in Czech-FB group
Black Expats in Czech Republic

Prague

Restaurants

Afro Community Center and
Bistro
Kateřinská 485/20 128 00
Prague, Czech Republic

Denmark

There is no specific "Black
Dane" community but there are
black people in Denmark.
Denmark is accepting of all
people so you won't experience
anything out of the ordinary while
visiting.
Black Americans in Copenhagen
Black Womxn and Black Non-
Binary People in Copenhagen

Couleur Cafe- African Music
Celebration in June

Copenhagen

Beauty/Cosmetics

Nyah Beauty
Rantzausgade 8b 2200
Copenhagen, Denmark

Restaurants

Ma'ed
Griffenfeldsgade 7,
2200 København, Denmark

SASAA
blågårdsgade 2 A 2200

Copenhagen, Denmark
http://www.sasaa.dk/

The Caribbean Housewife
Skydebanegade 3
Copenhagen, Denmark 1709
http://thecaribbeanhousewife.co
m/
UGood
Jægersborggade 39
2200 Copenhagen, Denmark
+45 52 39 96 91

Yam CPH
Central Station shopping center
Station
Square 7, Copenhagen Denmark

Salons/ Barbershops

Bernard The Barber
Vesterbrogade 91E
1620 KBH, V
+45.22399314

Barikisu Hair Academy
Vesterbrogade 102
DK - 1620, Kbh V
Denmark

Afro hair and Body Shop
Fredensgade 17 2200
Copenhagen, Denmark

Haddy's Hair and Beauty Shop
valby-langgade 122 2500
Valby, Denmark

Riiam's Braids
riamsbraids@gmail.com

Continents/Countries

Afro Benidan
Gasværksvej 19 A,
1656 Copenhagen, Denmark

Creation of beauty salon
Bjergegade 7 3000
Copenhagen, Denmark

Afromeri Beauty Supply
Istedgade 13 1650
Copenhagen, Denmark

Tour

"I Am Queen Mary" statue
The Danish West Indian
Warehouse
https://www.iamqueenmary.com/

Wellness

ConfidentGains
@thewelbodicoach

Yema Ferreira Psychotherapy
and Coaching
contact@yemaferreira.com
https://www.yemaferreira.com/

Estonia

Although very few you will find
Black families in Talinn . You
won't experience racism here,
but travel alert and aware.

Finland

Is home to about 50k black
people. A lot of them were born
there and are referred to as
"Afro Finns" .

Afro Finns organization
https://afrofinns.com/

Black Hair Event: Good Hair Day
- August

Helsinki

Grocery

Mini Ethio Market
Käenkuja 4 A 2 00500
Helsinki, Finland

Samson's African & Oriental
food
Haapaniemenkatu 1,
00530 Helsinki, Finland

Restaurants

Addis Ethiopian Kitchen
Sturenkatu 28 00510
Helsinki, Finland

African Pots
Mäkelänkatu 45 C 00550
Helsinki, Finland
http://www.africanpots.fi/

John's Coffee
Mall of Tripla
Firdonkatu 2
00520 Helsinki

Salons/Barbershops

Kinaporinkatu 1, 00500 Helsinki,
Finland

France- France is full of Black people throughout the country. There is said to be between 3-5 million. Although there is no overt racism Black people still deal with bias and microaggressions.

Lyon

Beauty/Cosmetics

Makeup by Ilona
91 avenue Francis de Pressensé
69200 Vénissieux France
+33 6 43 34 94 49

Restaurants

Africa Food Concept
14 Grande rue de la Guillotière
69007 Lyon, France
Le Conarky
112 Grande rue de la Guillotière
69007 Lyon,France

Chez Magie
19 Rue Creuzet
69007 Lyon France
Afrikavaise
39b rue Saint-Pierre de Vaise
69009 Lyon,France

Lyon Dakar
227 Rue Créqui
69003 Lyon, France

Tante Lina
24 rue René Leynaud
69001 Lyon ,France

Mattsam

85 rue Massena,
69006 Lyon, France

La Mangue Amere
7 rue du Jardin des Plantes,
69001 Lyon, France

Afrika Burger
36 cours de Verdun Perrache
Rez de
Chausse, 69002 Lyon, France

Africain La Symbiose
85 avenue Berthelot,
69007 Lyon, France

Restaurant Africana
44 grande rue de la guillotiere
69007 Lyon, France

Salons/Barbershops

Afro Look Coiffure
26 grande rue de la Guillotière
Lyon, France 69007

Barber Designer
2 Rue d'Algérie,
69001 Lyon, France

Mahenna Ana
67 Grande Rue de la Guillotière,
69007 Lyon, France

Best Afro Salon de Coiffure
Mixte
100 Grande Rue de la
Guillotière,
69007 Lyon, France

Manuela Beauty Black

Continents/Countries

316 Rue Garibaldi,
69007 Lyon, France

Black Pearl
1 Avenue Félix Faure,
69007 Lyon, France

Marseille
Restaurant
IVOIRE
57 Rue d'Aubagne,
13001 Marseille, France

Mame Diarra
l'académie, 30 Rue de
l'Académie, 13001
Marseille, France

Salon Volodia
44 rue de l'eveché
13002 Marseille, France

Le Chaudron Africain
27 RUE ADOLPHE THIERS
13001
Marseille, France

La Jungle
22 Rue Chateauredon,
13001 Marseille, France

Black Friday Restaurant
60 Rue d'Aubagne,
13001 Marseille, France

À l'Île de la Réunion Restaurant
14 Rue de la Paix Marcel Paul,
13001 Marseille, France

Salons/Barbershops

Future Line Afro
8 Rue Rouvière,
13001 Marseille, France

Afro Star
13 rue du Marché des Capucins
13001 Marseille, France

New Star African American
26, rue de la Palud
13001 Marseille, France
Montpellier

Restaurants

Restaurant Saveurs d'Afrique
11 Rue Henri René,
34000 Montpellier, France

Delices Africa
4 Rue Bourrely,
34000 Montpellier, France

Le maquis
20 Rue de la Méditerranée,
 34070 Montpellier, France

Salons/Barbershops

Tresses sur Montpellier
611 rue saint priest
340000 Montpellier, France

Royal Hair and Beauty
7 Boulevard du Jeu de Paume,
34000 Montpellier, France

Astou Espace Beaute
34 Rue du Faubourg du
Courreau,
34000 Montpellier, France

HBC Coiffure
18 Rue d'Alger,
34000 Montpellier, France

Styl Hair
5 Rue d'Alsace,
34000 Montpellier, France

Grace Ivoire
5 Rue du Clos René,
34000 Montpellier, France

Senegal Beauty
4 Rue du Pont de Lattes,
34000 Montpellier, France

Villleurbanne

Restaurant

Afripeen
2 avenue Salvador Allende,
69100 Villeurbanne France

MAMA CÉLÉ | AFRICAN FOOD
Mamacele.fr
+33 7 78 36 51 44

Salons/Barbershops

Ehyram
76 Rue Anatole France,
69100 Villeurbanne, France

Dile Creation
37 Rue des Charmettes,
69100 Villeurbanne, France

Salon Michigan
51 cours tolstoi (5,803.01 mi)

Villeurbanne, France 69100

Paris

As we know Paris has a large amount of Afro-Parisians. Our businesses can be found in many Arrondissements. Specific Black Neighborhoods are Strasbourg– Saint-Denis and Chateau D'eau.
https://www.entreetoblackparis.com/

Beauty/Cosmetics

Le Curl Shop

Online shop with tons of products

Nail Xperience-2 Locations
2nd floor Citadium Caumartin, 56 rue caumartin 75009 / Metro Caumartin / Saint Lazare / Auber
10 rue mesnil / Metro 2 Victor Hugo

Prestige 55
55 Rue du Château d'Eau, 75010

Colorful Black
7 Rue Poissonnière, 75002

MGC International
29 Boulevard de Strasbourg, 75010 or 1-3
Paris, France

A.B.S Afro Cosmetics

Continents/Countries

9 Rue de Clignancourt, 75018
Paris

Aramozone
 25 Rue de l'École de Médecine,
75006

Bookstores
Présence Africaine
25 bis rue des Ecoles
75005 Paris, FR

Events

Brown Sugar Days - Summer
series
Afro Punk- July

Restaurants

Gumbo YaYa Chicken and
Waffles
3 Rue Charles Robin,
75010 Paris, France

Waly-Fay
6 Rue Godefroy Cavaignac
 75011 Paris, France (11th)

Afrikin Fusion - Multiple locations

1. 330 Rue des Pyrénées,
75020 Paris, France (18th)

2.28 Avenue de Saint-Ouen,
75018 Paris, France (17th)

3.54 Rue Jeanne d'Arc,
 75013 Paris, France (13th)

Ménélik

4 Rue Sauffroy,
75017 Paris, France (17th)

Osè
34 Rue du Faubourg Saint-
Martin,
75010 Paris, France (10th)

L'Équateur
151 Rue Saint-Maur,
75011 Paris, France (11th)

Ohinene
14 Rue de la Chine,
75020 Paris, France (20th)

Le 404
69 Rue des Gravilliers,
75003 Paris, France (3rd)

Le Petit Dakar
6 Rue Elzevir,
75003 Paris, France (3rd)

Le Comptoir General
80 Quai de Jemmapes,
75010 Paris, France

Sunday in Soho
7 Rue Saint-Marc,
75002 Paris, France (3rd)

Mama Jackson's Soul Food
12 Rue Claude Tillier,
75012 Paris, France (12th)

BMK Paris
14 Rue de la Fidélité,
75010 Paris, France (10th)

Jah Jah

11 Rue des Petites Écuries,
 75010 Paris, France (10th)

Bô
8 Rue de Poissy,
75005 Paris, France (5TH)

Baieta
5 Rue de Pontoise,
75005 Paris, France (5th)

O'maki
65 Rue Letort,
75018 Paris, France

Boulom
181 Rue Ordener,
75018 Paris, France

Le Maquis
53 Rue des Cloys,
75018 Paris, France

La Villa Massai
9 Boulevard des Italiens,
75002 Paris, France (1st)

Babylone Bis
34 rue tiquetonne
75002 Paris, France

Salons/Barbershops -

Main Area for hair appointments
Chateau Rouge.

Hair Events

Natural Hair Academy- Annual
conference since 2013 dedicated
to natural hair. This year's

conference will take place June
9th.

Black Beauty University: Online
coaching platform created by
Clarise Libenne that is
dedicated to all types of natural
hair.

Ma Coiffeuse Afro– Is a mobile
application that connects women
with afro hair to stylists in Paris
that will come to your home or
you can go to a salon. All the
stylists are hand picked,
professional, and have
undergone quality assurance to
ensure they are able to do the
hair styles advertised on the
app(braids, blow-outs, hair cuts,
color, etc).

Nappy Days– is dedicated to
hosting events for Natural hair in
Paris. The also host a "Miss
Nappy" pageant
un-Ruly– is an online community
that celebrates and inspires the
versatility and beauty of Black
hair and women. They have an
awesome series called Pretty
which examines the ideas of
what beauty means in different
parts of the world. Check out the
Paris series for Paris.

Ma Coiffeuse Afro
10 rue de penthièvre
 75008 Paris, France

Afro Soins

47 Rue Championnet, 75018

Salon D
5 rue Léon Jouhaux, 75010
07 77 70 75 58

Nicole Pembrook
nicpembrook@gmail.com
+33 6 66 62 65 71

Ciara Coiffure
http://ciara-coiffure.com/
@ciaracoiffure

Daba Fashion 2
1 rue Montcalm, 75018
+33 9 52 95 41 29

Djeneba
+33 6 44 70 55 17

Polished Hair
76-78 avenue de Champs
Elysees

75008 Paris, France

Belle Et Nubian's
5 Rue la Condamine,
75017 Paris

Black spoon- Food Truck
Le-Tricycle- Food Bike

Tours

Little Africa Tour
http://www.littleafrica.fr/
@littleafricaparis

Black paris Tour
http://www.blackparistour.com/
@blackparistours

Entre to Black Paris- Josephine Baker Tour
https://www.entreetoblackparis.com/
paris@entreetoblackparis.com

Le Paris Noir
http://leparisnoir.com/
@leparisnoir

Girl meets Glass wine tour
https://www.girlmeetsglass.com/
tanisha@girlmeetsglass.com

Wellness

Cooking with Class cooking class

Georgia - The majority of black people here are in Tbilisi as students. They will stare but they are friendly. Please visit aware and alert.

Germany

Afro Germans have been in the country since the 16th century. There is a large amount of Black people throughout Germany as Afro-Germans, immigrants and army officers. More than 1 million of people of African Descent live in Germany.

Community

GENERATION ADEFRA : Black
Women in Germany
Black Sisterhood Germany
Black Hair&Skin Berlin

Berlin

https://www.blackbrownberlin.co
m/

Cultural Center

Afropolitan Berlin
Möckernstraße 72, 1
0965 Berlin, Germany

Afrika Haus
Bochumer Str. 25,
10555 Berlin, Germany

Each one Teach one
Togostraße 76,
13351 Berlin, Germany

Restaurants

Attaya Cafe
Zelter Str. 6
10439 Berlin, Germany

Rosa Caleta
Muskauer Str. 9,
10997 Berlin, Germany

Tembo African Restaurant
Danckelmannstr .20
14059 Charlottenburg, Germany

Ya Man

Gotzkowskystraße 17
10555 Berlin, Germany

Madinina Délice Créole
Warschauer Straße 12,
10243 Berlin

Salons/Barbershops

Cocoon Hairshop
Potsdamer Str. 193
10783 Berlin

Afro Center Salon
Silbersteinstraße 71,
12051 Berlin, Germany

Martins Afro Style Shop
Potsdamer Straße 189,
10783 Berlin, Germany

Ebony and Ivory
Potsdamer Straße 158,
10783 Berlin, Germany

Afro Lydia Hair Salon
Goebenstraße 7,
10783 Berlin, Germany

GT World of Beauty
Joachimsthaler Str. 19,
10719 Berlin, Germany

Max Afro Shop
Karl-Marx-Straße 25,
12043 Berlin, Germany

Get Hair Afro Shop
Bredowstraße 48,
10551 Berlin, Germany

African Beauty Bazaar
Sesenheimer Str. 16,
10627 Berlin, Germany

Afro and Body Shop
Hobrechtstraße 2,
12043 Berlin, Germany

Kymani & King
Müllerstraße 97,
13349 Berlin, Germany

Jorostar Afro hair and Beauty
Brüsseler Str. 50,
13353 Berlin, Germany

Natural Hair Berlin
Nürnberger Str. 7,
10787 Berlin, Germany

Urban Sparkz Barber Shop
Sonnenalle 29,
12047 Berlin

Benny Barbers
Gervinusstr 19th
10629 , Berlin

Malaika Hair
Grolmanstr. 15
10623 Berlin, Germany

Bremen

Grocery

Makosa Afroshop
Falkenstraße 16,
28195 Bremen, Germany

Restaurants

Momies Corner
Langemarckstraße 128,
28199 Bremen, Germany

Mataa's Kitchen
Elisabethstraße 118,
 28217 Bremen, Germany

Christy's
Hankenstraße 27,
28195 Bremen, Germany

Salons/Barber Shops

Kuumba African Hair Salon
Langemarckstraße 171,
28199 Bremen, Germany

Pretty Lady Afro Hair
Rembertistraße 67
Bremen, Germany

Black Beauty
Waller Ring 133,
28219 Bremen, Germany

Cologne

Restaurants

Shaka Zulu
Limburger Str. 29,
50672 Köln, Germany
Africa Drum Nigerian Restaurant
Ebertpl. 1,
50668 Köln, Germany

Treasure African Restaurant
Mettmanner Str. 1,
40233 Düsseldorf, Germany

Injera Restaurants
Lindenstraße 86,
50674 Köln, Germany

Hdmona
Eburonenstraße 1,
50678 Köln, Germany

Selam
Ehrenfeldgürtel 91,
50823 Köln, Germany

Fasika
Luxemburger Str. 17,
50674 Köln, Germany

Just try Afro Soul Food- 2
locations
Location 1: Oskar-Jäger-Straße
52,
 Bei Netto Market

Location 2: Subbelrather str 242
₁
50825 Köln 50825 Cologne,
Germany

Salons/Barbershops

Margaret Afro Hairdressing
Frankfurter Str. 76,
51065 Köln, Germany

Afro-Friseur Salon Kathy Köln
Montanusstraße 1,
51065 Köln, Germany

Zadoo Afro Hair Shop
Breite Str. 83,
50667 Köln, Germany

Black and White Hair Salon
Frankfurter Str. 702,
51107 Köln, Germany

Zeebra Tropicana
Richard-Wagner-Str. 29,
50674 Köln, Germany

Professionelle Extensions
Noblestyle
Michele Njessi
+49 221 16847591

Ceforafrica
Luxemburger Str. 18,
50674 Köln, Germany

Lina Afro Hair Braiding
Schwabstraße 60,
70193 Stuttgart, Germany

Salem's Afro Salon
Gutleutstraße 155,
60327 Frankfurt am Main,
Germany

Black Hair Saloon
Gutleutstraße 127,
60327 Frankfurt am Main,
Germany

Darmstadt

Restaurants

Hi Kenkey House
+49 69 24246203

Baobab
Wenckstraße 1A,
64289 Darmstadt, Germany

124

Afrikanische Küche, speziell aus
Eritrea
Wenckstraße 1A,
64289 Darmstadt, Germany

Salons/Barbershops

King David Afroshop Darmstadt
Holzstraße 9,
64283 Darmstadt, Germany

Afroshop Cocoon
Kirchstraße 12,
64283 Darmstadt, Germany

Frankfurt

Restaurants

African Queen Restaurant
 Stuttgarter Str. 21,
60329 Frankfurt am Main,
Germany

Nollywood
Hafenstraße 19,
60327 Frankfurt am Main,
Germany

Mommona
Große Rittergasse 58,
60594 Frankfurt am Main,
Germany

Ethiopian
Leipziger Str. 47,
60487 Frankfurt am Main,
Germany

Sebeta
Werftstraße 15,

60327 Frankfurt am Main,
Germany

Diliet Bistro
Eschersheimer Landstraße 18,
60322 Frankfurt am Main,
Germany

Kilimanjaro Restaurant
Hafenstraße 52,
60327 Frankfurt am Main,
Germany

Ambassel
Deutschherrnufer 28,
60594 Frankfurt am Main,
Germany

African Hut
Alte G. 69,
60313 Frankfurt am Main,
Germany

African Hut Bistro
Koblenzer Str. 22,
60327 Frankfurt am Main,
Germany

Demera
Holzhausenstraße 77,
60322 Frankfurt am Main,
Germany

Salons/ Barbershops

Black Hair Salon
Gutleutstrasse 127
60327 Frankfurt, Germany

VIP Hair Salon
Düsseldorferstrasse 12

60329 Frankfurt, Germany

Salem's Afro Hair Salon
Gutleutstraße 155
60327 Frankfurt, Germany

Las Bonitas Hair and Nails
Kaiserstraße 60,
60329 Frankfurt am Main,
Germany

VIP Hair and braiding
Düsseldorfer Str. 12,
60329 Frankfurt am Main,
Germany

Jossy Hair Braiding
Koblenzerstr 6
60327 Frankfurt, Germany

Hamburg

Restaurants

Afrikanisches Bistro by Hadjia
Repsoldstraße 49,
20097 Hamburg, Germany

Papaye Restaurant
Afrikanisches
Stormarner Str. 1,
22049 Hamburg, Germany

Selam
Simrockstraße 186,
22589 Hamburg, Germany

Ghana Aba Abrokyire
Hammer Deich 10,
20537 Hamburg, Germany

Anni Spices

Sönke-Nissen-Allee 2A,
21509 Glinde, Germany

Afrika-Verein der deutschen
Wirtschaft
Neuer Jungfernstieg 21,
20354 Hamburg, Germany

Salons/Barbershops

SOUFI SALON

Wandsbeker Chaussee 182
22089 Hamburg Germany

Hamburg Briads
Swebenbrunnen
22159 Hamburg, Germany

Oliviera Work
Lange Reihe 30-32
20099 Hamburg, Germany

Munich

Restaurants

Makula
Dreimühlenstraße 14,
80469 München, Germany

Café Omo Äthiopisches
Restaurant
Zenettistraße 25,
80337 München, Germany

De Afric
Theresienstraße 146,
80333 München, Germany

Salons/Barbershops

Afro Kings and Ebony Beauty
Hermann-Lingg-Straße 2,
80336 München, Germany

Ethnic Hair and Beauty
Ungererstraße 80,
80805 München, Germany

Urembo
Behringstraße 10,
82152 Planegg, Germany

Greece

There is a native afro greek community that you can find in the Avato or thrace regions. Although not big in number many Nigerians have moved to Greece and raised families there.

Communities

Nigerian Community
Thessaloniki & The Northern
Greece- FB Group
Nigerian Community Greece- FB
Group

Athens

Specific Black community is
Sepolia

Restaurants

Yankadi
Lelas Karagianni 11,
Athina 112 52, Greece

Chri-Bri Bar restaurant. African's
grill
Pithias 2, Athina
113 64, Greece

Prestige African Restaurant
15, Spartis 11252,
Athina, Greece

POP-UP MAMA AFRICA
RESTAURANT
Sfaktirias 23,
Athina 104 35, Greece

Salons/Barbershops

Saloon Afrika
Mithimnis 30, Athina
112 57, Greece

Rita La Nagrita
Agias Lavras 12 Peristeri
12131 Athens, Greece

Erica Essence Hair
11527 Athens, Greece

Rasta kotsidakia All the Styles
Ψαρρων 12244 Athens, Greece

Hungary

There is a great resource found on Black girl in Budapest from the wonderful Starr who is a black expat. Her resource was used for this guide.

Restaurants

Sly's Coffee Shop & Bar
Budapest, Nagy Diófa u. 29,
1072 Hungary

Afrikai Bufe and Bar
Budapest, Bérkocsis u. 21,
1084 Hungary

Taste Brasil
+36 20 317 7481
tastebrasilbudapest@gmail.com

Mimi's Grill
@mimi_grill
+36 70 590 9730
Gidi 2 U
www.gidi2u.com
delivery@gidi2u.com
+36 30 333 8330

Lalibela Étterem
Jókai utca 40 Budapest,
 Hungary 1066

Yv's Kitchen- open for delivery
yvetteacho73@gmail.com

Lagos Büfé African Fast Foods
Budapest, Népszínház u. 42,
1081 Hungary

Qawa- Art of Coffee
Balzac u. 40 b Budapest,
Hungary 11136

Salons/ Barbershops

Afro Stilusok
https://afrostilusok.simplybook.it/

Afrostilusok@gmail.com

Francis Shop
Szalay u. 5a Budapest,
Hungary 1055

Beauty By Suti
meemeedanielk@gmail.com
@bb_suti

Unique Salon and Barbership
Rákóczi tér 11. Budapest,
Hungary 1084

Iceland - There is no longer the black owned restaurant , but there are black people in Iceland working in the major cities. You will get stares as a tourist from other tourist who have never seen a black person. It poses no threat but I have experienced being called a monkey walking down the street, so please proceed aware and alert

Italy

Afro Italians aren't large in numbers and are the children of native eritreans, ethiopians and somali's. There is a population of Nigerians and Kenyans, and you will see that reflected in markets and the restaurants listed below.

Bergamo

Restaurant

Dahlak Restaurant
 Via Borgo Palazzo, 82/l,

24125 Bergamo BG, Italy

Milan

Restaurants

Corey's Soul Kitchen
Via Paolo Sarpi,
53 20154 Milan, Italy

Ristorante Bar mamma Africa
 Via Giulio e Corrado Venini,
8/14, 20127 Milano MI, Italy
Ristorante baobab cucina
multietnica

Via Alessandro Tadino, 48,
20124 Milano MI, Italy

Balafon
Via Teodosio, 6,
20131 Milano MI, Italy

Mosobna
Via Alessandro Tadino, 9,
20124 Milano MI, Italy

Kings and Queen
Via Panfilo Castaldi, 28,
20124 Milano MI, Italy

Salons/Barbershops

Black Diamond
Via Panfilo Castaldi, 42,
20124 Milano MI, Italy
Capelli di Helen
Via Panfilo Castaldi, 21,
20124 Milano MI, Italy

Olbia

Restaurant

Mannar Touba Teranga
Via Fiume D'Italia, 23,
07026 Olbia SS, Italy

Rome

Restaurant

Enqutatash
Viale della Stazione Prenestina,
55, 00177 Roma RM, Italy
Sahara Restaurant
Viale Ippocrate, 43,
00161 Roma RM, Italy

Africa Restaurant
Via Gaeta, 26,
00185 Roma RM, Italy

Taverna Del Mossob
Via Prenestina, 109,
00100 Roma RM, Italy

Massawa Restaurant
Via Montebello, 28,
00185 Roma RM, Italy

Ristorante Eritrea
Piazza del Gazometro, 1,
00154 Roma RM, Italy

Asmara Restaurant
Via Cernaia, 36,
00185 Roma RM, Italy

Turin

Restaurant

Mar Rosso afro restaurant &
cafe
Via Silvio Pellico, 13/E,
10125 Torino TO, Italy

Ristorante Kilimangiaro
Via della Pineta, 67,
09125 Cagliari CA, Italy

Kosovo

When traveling to Kosovo you
might be the first black person
they've ever seen. Be prepared
for the stares, and women please
be aware of your surroundings.
Latvia- Less than 100 black
people here. Mainly Nigerian.
There is a saint, saint maurice
that you can find in the main
square that is of African origins.
Liechtenstein
Unfortunately I have no
information for this country, but
please travel alert and aware.

Lithuania

There are less than 300 black
people here, with the majority of
them being from Nigeria. You can
find them studying in Vilnius or
Kaunas.

Luxembourg

Racism is on higher alert in
Luxembourg according to the
black people that live there

Malta

Racism is on higher alert in Malta.
People of African descent
experience more issues and are
said to live in fear. Again these
are the opinions of residents and
not tourist.

Moldova

There are black people in
Maldova due to education and
asylum . Everyone is in Chisinau
and they suggest you stay there
and not in the villages.

Netherlands

Because the Dutch colonized
Aruba, Guyana and Suriname,
Black Dutch people are found
throughout the Netherlands in
large numbers. The Surinamese
communities have a huge
celebration on June and July 1. I
highly recommend creating your
trips around this time to
experience these events.
https://webuyblack.nl/ - Black
owned businesses database in
the Netherlands.

Almere

Restaurants

Neighbours Kitchen
Marie Curiestraat 3, 1341 CA
Almere, Netherlands

Finish your Breakfast
Schoutstraat 28, 1315 EX
Almere, Netherlands

Restaurant Jeanette
Belfort 5 - 7, 1315 VA
Almere, Netherlands

Salons/Barbarshops
She Ross Hair
Europalaan 921, 1363 BM
Almere Poort, Netherlands

Afro Curls Beauty Salon
Sumatraweg 5, 1335 JM
Almere, Netherlands

Pak Afro Cosmetics
Bottelaarpassage 69, 1315 EP
Almere, Netherlands

Amsterdam

Communities

Amsterdam Black Woman-
outstanding organization for
expats.
Amsterdam Bijlmer is a
predominantly black
neighborhood

Accommodation

Hostelle
Bijlmerplein 395,
1102 DK Amsterdam,
Netherlands

Museums

The Black Archives
Zeeburgerdijk 19b
The Black Archives is located in
the historic
building of Vereniging Ons
Suriname.

Restaurants

African Kitchen
Wisseloord 85, 1107 NB
Amsterdam, Netherlands

Red's Kitchen
Bijlmerplein 110-111, 1102 DB
Amsterdam-Zuidoost,
Netherlands
TerraZen Centre
Sint Jacobsstraat 19HS,
 1012 NC Amsterdam

Labryinth
Amstelveenseweg 53, 1075 VT
 Amsterdam, Netherlands

Raggae Ritas
Nieuwe Kerkstraat 84, 1018 EC
Amsterdam, Netherlands

Water and Brood
Nieuwe Kerkstraat 84, 1018 EC
Amsterdam, Netherlands

African Black Star Coffee Shop
Rozengracht 1-A, 1016 LP
Amsterdam, Netherlands

Vle's Kitchen
Develstein 100C,
1102 AK Amsterdam,
Netherlands

Rotishop Gieta Surinamese
Balboastraat 15HS, 1057 VS
Amsterdam, Netherlands

Warung Swietie Lelydorp
Eerste Sweelinckstraat 1, 1073
CK
Amsterdam, Netherlands

De Hapjeshoek
Metrostation, Waterlooplein 6,
1011 MS
Amsterdam, Netherlands

Spice Course Amsterdam
Tweede Keucheniusstraat 12,
1051 VR
Amsterdam, Netherlands

Tjon Express
Buikslotermeerplein 63, 1025 ES
Amsterdam, Netherlands

Cereal and Chill
Dusartstraat 22, 1072 HS
Amsterdam, Netherlands

Mooshka
Van Woustraat 110, 1073 LL
Amsterdam, Netherlands

Queen D's
Develstein 100 1102 AK
Amsterdam, Netherlands

De Pom Bar
Cabralstraat 49h, 1057 CE
Amsterdam, Netherlands

My Broodje
Jan Pieter Heijestraat 98, 1053
GT
Amsterdam, Netherlands

Yemana
Reigersbos 3A, 1106 AP
Amsterdam, Netherlands

Salons/Barbershops

The Natural Nation
Zaanstraat 109,
1013 RW Amsterdam,
Netherlands

Annie's Place

Agatha Christiesingel 28, 1102
WK
Amsterdam, Netherlands

The Hair and Body Shop
Albert Cuypstraat 225, 1073 BG
Amsterdam, Netherlands

Saman Afro Beauty
Kinkerstraat 202, 1053 EL
Amsterdam, Netherlands

Beauty Salon Magic
Rijnstraat 218, 1079 HT
Amsterdam, Netherlands

Lara Afro Cosmetics
Javastraat 61, 1094 HA
Amsterdam, Netherlands

Afro Beauty Salon
Bijlmerplein 522, 1102 DP
Amsterdam, Netherlands

Sweets/Bakery

No No Cakes
http://www.nonocakes.com/

Tours
Black Heritage Tours
http://www.blackheritagetours.com/

The Hague

Restaurant

Casa de Sabor
Torenstraat 32, 2513 BS
 Den Haag, Netherlands

3 Stones
Laan van Meerdervoort 46 a,
 2517 AM Den Haag,
Netherlands

Koshina Nos Kultura
Pletterijstraat 1, 2515 AZ
 Den Haag, Netherlands

Rotterdam
Beauty/Cosmetics
Finesse MUA
https://www.finessemua.com/

Restaurants

Freddy's Comfort Food
Rotterdam
Vierambachtsstraat 145b, 3022 AL
Rotterdam, Netherlands

Sushi Order
Kralinger Esch 2, 3063 NB
Rotterdam, Netherlands

Noah Bar and Restaurant
Wijnhaven 3A Ingang
Gelderseplein, 3011
WG Rotterdam, Netherlands

Coco Rotterdam
Hoogstraat 45, 3011 PE
Rotterdam, Netherlands
Fred and Harrys
Noorderweg 22a, 3119 XX
Schiedam, Netherlands

Pasta N' Casa
Pastancasa.com

Spikizi
Zwarte Paardenstraat 91a,
3012 VK Rotterdam

Sweets/Bakery

Kandy Krush
Mauritsweg 60, 3012 JX
Rotterdam, Netherlands

Zandaam

Beauty/Cosmetics

Teshura Teshura.nl

Provincialeweg 302 / Unit 265
1506 MJ Zaandam

Salons/Barbershops

Black Queen Hair and
Cosmetics
Nieuwe Binnenweg 223A, 3021
GC
Rotterdam, Netherlands

Afro Beauty Planet
Voermanweg 896, 3067 JW
Rotterdam, Netherlands

Afro Beauty Shop
Oude Watering 181, 3077 RG
Rotterdam, Netherlands

North Macedonia

(formerly Macedonia)- A safe
country for black tourist. They
are very hospitable and are
ready to welcome all.

Norway- The black population
here is referred to as Afro
Norweigian or Afro-Norsk The
majority of black people are
somali with the others hailing
fromvEritrea, Ethiopia, Sudan.
The majority of black people can
be found in Oslo.

Oslo

Restaurants

Waaberi
Platous gate 6, 0190
Oslo, Norway

House of Africa
Storgata 41, 0182
Oslo, Norway

Hakuna Matata
Møllergata 38, 0179
Oslo, Norway

Mesob
Motzfeldts gate 5, 0187
Oslo, Norway

Salons/Barbershops

Royal Afro Hair Salon
Brugata 17b, 0186
Oslo, Norway

Becs Afro Hair Salon
Skippergata 33, 0154
Oslo, Norway

Studio Africa
Bogstadveien 51, 0366
Oslo, Norway

TS Afro Hair Salon
Calmeyers gate 7 A/B, 0183
Oslo, Norway

Kejetia African Supermarket &
Saloon DA
Trondheimsveien 5, 0560
Oslo, Norway

Braid beyond
Ullevålsveien 1, 0165
Oslo, Norway

Bobby's Hair and cosmetics
Dronningens Gate 28, 0154

Oslo, Norway

Poland

There are around 5k black people in Poland and you can find them in the cities of Warsaw (Wola), Łódź, Wrocław, Gdańsk, Szczecin. They are still heavily discriminate against and be called Monkey or Ni**** walking down the street.

Communities

Being Black In Poland- FB group
Strangers at the gate: Black Poland- FB group
All Africans in Poland- FB group

Grocery

African Hair and Food supply service
+48-507-247-292
office@afroeuro.pl

Restaurants

African Kitchen
Braci Wagów 20, 00-001
Warszawa, Poland

Portugal

Afro-Portuguese predominately hail from Angola, Cape Verde, Guinea-Bissau, Mozambique and São Tomé and Príncipe.

Lisbon

Quinta do Mochhas is the predominantly black neighborhood

Grocery

Calçada do Garcia

Restaurants

Cantinho do Aziz
R. de São Lourenço 5,
1100-530 Lisboa, Portugal

Restaurante Moçambicano Roda Viva
Beco do Mexias, 11 R/C 1100-349
Alfama, Portugal

Djairsound
Rua dasJanelas Verdes n° 22
1200-691
 Lisbon, Portugal

Casa de Angola
Travessa da Fábrica das Sedas 7,
1250-096 Lisboa, Portugal

Cantinho do Aziz
 R. de São Lourenço 5,
1100-530 Lisboa, Portugal

Estrela Morena
R. da Imprensa Nacional 64A,
Lisboa, Portugal

Restaurante Mwana Pwo

R. do Bojador 65, 1990-254
Lisboa, Portugal

Mulemba X'Angola
Largo José Afonso,
Olival Basto, Portugal

Tambarina
R. do Poço dos Negros 94,
1200-109 Lisboa, Portugal

Restaurante Anastácia -
Sabores
R. do Poço dos Negros 64,
1200-109 Lisboa, Portugal

Roda Viva
Beco do Mexias 11 R/c, 1100-
349
Lisboa, Portugal

Salons/Barbershops

Afro Braids Lisboa
Av. Padre Bartolomeu de
Gusmão 11C,
2720-425 Damaia, Portugal

Tranças Africanas by Cadija
R. Eng. Maciel Chaves 9A,
1900-269 Lisboa, Portugal

Barsha Beauty
R. do Arco do Marquês de
Alegrete 4D,
1100-034 Lisboa, Portugal

Délia - Cabelos Afro e Europeus
R. Movimento das Forças
Armadas 31A,

2845-380 Amora, Portugal

Tours

African Lisbon Tours - Naky
https://africanlisbontour.com/

Guias da Quinta do Mocho
Walking Grafitti tour

Wine Experience

Sommerlier Cha McKoy is
gracing lisbon with her wine
knowledge and experience! One
of the only Black Sommliers
globally booking her while there
you're in Portugal is a MUST.

https://www.chamccoy.com/

Romania

All though there's a small number
of black people in Romania the
majority is there to study. You can
find them in major cities including:
Bucharest, Cluj-Napoca,
Timişoara, Iaşi, Craiova,
Constanţa, Oradea. Expect
stares but nothing to be cautious
about.

Russia

There are about 50k Afro-
russians throughout the country
and they can be found in the
following cities: Moscow, St.
Petersburg, Rostov-on-Don,
Oryol, Lipetsk, Astrakhan . The

136

majority are, Nigerian, Ghanian, Cameroonian and Congolese. The reviews are mixed in terms of how black people are treated. I would suggest if you travel to Russia be alert and aware like you would any other country.

Moscow

Restaurants

Gerry Party People
Раушская набережная, д.
4 Moscow, Russia

La Cabana Africana
ул.Миклухо-Маклая 11Б
 Moscow, Russia 121500

NQ Foods
Ulitsa Marshala Savitskogo, 32,
Moscow, Russia, 117148

Bungalo
Zemlyanoy Val St, 6,
 Moscow, Russia, 105064

St.Petersburg

Community

Nigerian Community in Russia,
St. Petersburg

San Marino- The 3rd smallest country in Europe is safe for black people. Most black people who come through are tourist.

Serbia- Doesn't have a racially charged culture. They are said to be very friendly to all foreigners and tourist and will make sure you feel at home.

Slovakia-Although small in number most black people can be found in Bratislava. Their attitude towards tourist and foreigners are friendly.

Slovenia- This country is safe for black students and tourist. Ljubljana is full of people from all over the world. Black people are welcome here.

Spain- There are Afro-Spaniards that are originally from Equatorial Guinea. A Lot of Brazilians and Dominicans are in Spain as well. It is not out of the ordinary to see a Black person in Spain.

Community

Las Morenas De España- Your go to FB group for black expats.

Barcelona

Restaurants

Foni Africa Bar and Restaurant
Carrer de l'Est, 9,
08001 Barcelona, Spain

Eat Caribbean
Carrer de Montserrat, 4,
 08001 Barcelona, Spain

Le Saraba
C. de Villarroel, 30,
08011 Barcelona, Spain

Salons/Barbershops

Peluqueria iletnic
Carrer de Ramon Albó, 67, 08027
Barcelona, Spain

Madrid

Madrid is a welcoming city to black and brown people. Lavapiés is the place where you will find people that look like you, as well as hair shops. There is a high number of Dominicans in Cuatro Caminos a place you will also get authentic food and hair options.

Restaurants

La Pasa Bar Gin
Calle de San Bernardo, 73,
28015 Madrid, Spain

Restaurante Dakar
Calle del Amparo, 61,
28012 Madrid, Spain

El Mandela
Calle de la Independencia, 1,
28013 Madrid, Spain

Bazar El Menara
Calle del Mesón de Paredes, 61,
28012 Madrid, Spain

Sankara Lounge Bar
Cuesta de Sto. Domingo,
28013 Madrid, Spain

Restaurante Etiope Nuria
C. de Manuela Malasaña, 6,
28004 Madrid, Spain

Bar Colores Comida Senegal
Calle del Mesón de Paredes, 43,
28012 Madrid, Spain

Salons/ Barbershops

Shimada Kemp
Calle del Cardenal Cisneros, 8,
28010 Madrid, Spain

Guinea Peluquería
Calle del Amparo, 86,
28012 Madrid, Spain

Peluqueria Afro Latino
Calle del Mesón de Paredes, 80
28012 Madrid España

Afro Barber Fapenda
Calle del Amparo, 79,
28012 Madrid, Spain

Afro Naturals
info@afronatural.es
+34 698 22 53 46

Sweden

There are 200k+ Afro-Sweds and there is a vibrant community throughout. This term came to be in 1990

Stockholm
Rinkeby and Tensta is a neighborhood where you can find the black population. The police released a statement that these are Stockholms most "venerable areas" but this is where I saw myself, and I felt completely safe.

Beauty/Cosmetics

Barbara Mensah
https://www.barbaramensah.dk/
+45 53 56 45 04

Afro Drottning - Genet
Fridhemsgatan 38, 112 40
Stockholm, Sweden

Afro hair Academy Salon
Elizabeth
Tegnérgatan 45, 111 61
Stockholm, Sweden

Red Sea Afro Beauty
Surbrunnsgatan 50, 113 48
Stockholm, Sweden

Tnh77 Afro salon
Kungsholms strand 169
112 48 Stockholm, Sweden

Rosa Africa Sweden
Valstavägen 32C, 195 50
Märsta, Sweden

Luwam Afro Cosmetics and Cloth
Vårbergstorget 12, 127 43
Skärholmen, Sweden

Grocery

Visons Shop AB
Repslagargatan 6, 118 46
Stockholm, Sweden

Restaurants

Abyssinia Karlbergsvägen 46B,
113 37 Stockholm
http://abyssinia.se/Kontakt.html

Rutasoka Aröds industriväg 56
422 43 Hisings Backa
Telefon: 031-797 21 14

Jubba Restaurant
Helsingforsgatan 2,
164 78 Kista, Sweden

New Mama Africa R& B
Kista Bussterminalen under tunnelbana,
Danmarksgatan 19, 164 53
Kista, Sweden

Gojo
Renstiernas gata 48, 116 31
Stockholm, Sweden

Rutasoka Coffee
Aröds industriväg 56,
422 43 Hisings Backa, Sweden
Switzerland- There are around 75k+ black people in Switzerland. Those born and raised there are referred to as "Afro Swiss". The majority of black inhabits can be found in Basel, Geneva and Zurich.

Communities

African Heritage Switzerland- FB page

Afro Swiss- FB page

Afro Swiss Network-FB page

BExCH - Black Excellence Switzerland- FB page

Basel

Restaurants

EASTAFRO Restaurant Bahnhof SBB
Küchengasse 7, 4051
Basel, Switzerland

Abyssinia
Steinentorberg 26, 4051
Basel, Switzerland

Habesha
Markgräflerstrasse 89, 4057
Basel, Switzerland

Caribbean House
Viaduktstrasse 10, 4051
Basel, Switzerland

Barbershop/Salon

Goddess Braids
Güterstrasse 172, 4053
Basel, Switzerland

Bern

African Music Festival-
November

Restaurants

Injera
Gesellschaftsstrasse 38, 3012
Bern, Switzerland

Abysinnia
Seftigenstrasse 32, 3007
Bern, Switzerland

Café-Bar Bär im City-West
Laupenstrasse 19,
3008 Bern, Switzerland

Barbershop/Salon

Coiffeursalon FB Barber Shop
Moserstrasse 28, 3014
Bern, Switzerland

Black Lady Salon
Steinenbachgässlein 25, 4051
Basel, Switzerland

Afro-Diva-Beaute
Aarbergstrasse 119, 2502
Biel, Switzerland

Geneva

Restaurants

Africa Food Restaurant
Rue de Zurich 32, 1201
Genève, Switzerland

Le Pompadour, D. Diakwomo
Kina
Rue du Prieuré 22, 1202
Genève, Switzerland

Continents/Countries

Meskerem
Rue de Carouge 77, 1205
Genève, Switzerland

Aux 5 Sens
Rue de Montbrillant 20, 1201
Genève, Switzerland

L'awale Afro fusion
rue du Clos 15
1207 Geneva

La Couronne d'Or
Quai du Seujet 36, 1201
Genève, Switzerland

Fhoenix Cafe
Rue des Pâquis 11, 1201
Genève, Switzerland

Red Sea
Rue de Montbrillant 4, 1201
Genève, Switzerland

Asyrah Sismondi (Specialiste
Coiffure)
Rue Sismondi 7, 1201
Genève, Switzerland

Desi Cheril - Salon de coiffure
afro
rue du mole, le pâquis 42, 1201
Genève, Switzerland

Inside Africa Akwaaba
Place de Montbrillant 4, 1201
Genève, Switzerland

Zurich-You can find a large
number of black residence in the
langstrasse neighborhood

Communities

Black Film Festival Zurich
African Fashion Festival Zurich

Restaurants

Queen Idia African Restaurant &
Bar
Badenerstrasse 125, 8004
Zürich, Switzerland

African Queen
Stampfenbachstrasse 70, 8006
Zürich, Switzerland

Meskerem
Birmensdorferstrasse 364, 8055
Zürich, Switzerland

Mesob
Rotachstrasse 33, 8003
Zürich, Switzerland

African Delicious Food
Georg-Kempf-Strasse 10, 8046
Zürich, Switzerland

Haile House - Ethiopian Pop-Up

Universitätstrasse 23, 8006
Zürich, Switzerland

Filfl
Zentralstrasse 136,
8003 Zürich, Switzerland

Salons/ Barbershops

Jollof Beauty | Afro Braiding
Salon
Herrligstrasse 31, 8048
Zürich, Switzerland

Afro Shop Anice Hairstyle Black
& White
Klingenstrasse 39, 8005
Zürich, Switzerland

Afro Shop Sow
Stampfenbachstrasse 78, 8006
Zürich, Switzerland

Forester Beauty
Hagenholzstrasse 86
8050 Zürich Switzerland

Ukraine- Native Afro-Ukrainians
can be found in Kharkiv, Kiev,
Odessa .There are about 50k
African students who are from
West Africa and study medicine.
They celebrate Africa Day on
May 25 annually and celebrate
all African Countries during this
occasion.

Communities

African Council in Ukraine-
Community orginzations

Kyiv

Beauty Cosmetics

Fiducia
Aviakonstruktora Antonova St,
4/1,
Kyiv, Ukraine, 03186

Restaurants

Alisef
Martyrosyana St, 4,
Kyiv, Ukraine, 02000

Ibrange
Vadyma Hetmana St, 2,
Kyiv, Ukraine, 02000

Fiducia African Product Ukraine
Aviakonstruktora Antonova St,
4/1
Kyiv, Ukraine, 03186

Salons/Barbershops

Edy hair Planet
Harmatna St, 26/2,
Kyiv, Ukraine, 02000

Lviv

African Shop Ukraine
Lychakivska St, 31,
Lviv, Lviv Oblast, Ukraine, 79000

Vatican City

Besides the one Black priest that
lives here, Black travelers will
not experience any racism.

THE UK

October is Black History Month for the UK
https://www.blackhistorymonth.org.uk/
https://www.ukblackowned.co.uk/

African grocery delivery
www.olumofoods.co.

ENGLAND

BIRMINGHAM

Handsworth is a predominantly black neighborhood

Restaurants

24 Karat Bistro
 27 Warstone Ln, Birmingham
B18 6JQ, United Kingdom
24caratbistro.co.uk

Adians Restaurant
310-312 LADYPOOL ROAD,
BIRMINGHAM, B12 8JY
Adiansdining.co.uk
+44 121 449 9994

Afrikana
359 Ladypool Rd, Balsall Heath, Birmingham
B12 8LA, United Kingdom
+44 121 439 8118

Bantu
5-11 Fleet St, Birmingham
B3 1JP, United Kingdom

bantubirmingham.com
+44 121 212 2688

Glorious
Unit 3, 310 Summer Ln, Birmingham
B19 3RH, United Kingdom
+44 330 128 0900

Klassic Grill Bar
110 Icknield St, Birmingham
B18 6RZ, United Kingdom
+44 121 293 9372

Divine African and Caribbean Restaurant
325 Soho Rd, Birmingham
B21 9SD, United Kingdom
Divineafricanandcarribean.co.uk

Hamaran
461 Bearwood Rd, Bearwood, Birmingham,
Smethwick B66 4DH, United Kingdom
+44 121 792 3975

Kindia Africa Food
279 Dudley Rd, Birmingham
B18 4HA, United Kingdom
+44 121 439 8087

Petite Afrique
160 Hockley Hill, Birmingham
B18 5AN, United Kingdom

Prestige
42 Summer Hill Rd, Birmingham
B1 3RB, United Kingdom
+44 121 236 3188

Nakira
74 John Bright St, Birmingham
B1 1BN, United Kingdom
+44 121 643 1336

Savanna
32 Bristol St, Birmingham
B5 7AA, United Kingdom
+44 121 293 2174

Titanic
293 Birchfield Rd, Handsworth,
Birmingham
B20 3BX, United Kingdom

Tropical Delights
88-90 Vittoria St, Birmingham
B1 3PA, United Kingdom

Out of Africa
353 A Birchfield Rd,
Handsworth, Birmingham
B20 3BJ, United Kingdom
+44 121 356 1551

Salons/Barbershops

Box Braids By Leesa
+44 121 517 0291

Devine
398 Bearwood Rd, Bearwood,
Birmingham,
Smethwick B66 4EX, United
Kingdom
+44 121 420 3777

Freedom Edge
256 Dudley Road, Birmingham
B18 4HN

The ABC Travel Greenbook

Freedomedge.co.uk

Klassics Koncepts
9 Lower Severn St, Birmingham
B1 1PU, United Kingdom
https://www.blackhairbirmingham
.com/

Smart Cutz Barbers
138 Sandon Rd, Bearwood,
Birmingham
B66 4AB, United Kingdom

Stylers
39 Station Rd, Erdington,
Birmingham
B23 6UE, United Kingdom
+44 7832 530789

Tegur
45 Coopers Rd, Birmingham
B20 2JU, United Kingdom
+44 121 523 5979

Tia's locs and hair
15 York Rd, Birmingham
B23 6TE, United Kingdom
+44 121 377 8255

Tours

Black Heritage walks network
www.recognizeonline.com/tags/b
lack-heritage-walks-networks

Black History Walks
https://www.blackhistorywalks.co
.uk/

BRISTOL

Stokes Croft: St.Pauls, Bristol is the predominantly black neighborhood

St.Pauls Carnival- July

Restaurants

Agape house cafe and African food
99 Fishponds Rd, Eastville, Bristol BS5 6PN, United Kingdom

African Village Barbecue
406 Stapleton Rd, Easton, Bristol BS5 6NQ, United Kingdom

Bikkle Island
402 Stapleton Rd, Easton, Bristol BS5 6NQ, United Kingdom

Bravo's English and Caribbean Takeaway
215 Stapleton Rd, Easton, Bristol BS5 0PD, United Kingdom
+44 117 239 3709

Cafe Conscious
182 Avonvale Rd, Redfield, Bristol BS5 9SX, United Kingdom
+44 117 955 7883

Calypso Kitchen
Unit 3 Gaol Ferry Steps,

Bristol BS1 6WE, United Kingdom
+44 117 329 1314

Caribbean Croft
30 Stokes Croft, St Paul's, Bristol BS1 3QD
+44 0117 330 5298
Caribbeancroft.co.uk

Caribbean Wrap
Unit 33, St Nicholas Market, Bristol BS1 1JQ, United Kingdom
+44 7989 745944

Dine at Dayzeeks
31 Brislington Hill, Brislington, Bristol BS4 5BE, United Kingdom
+44 117 329 4200

Fi Real
57 West Street, Old Market, Bristol BS2 0BZ, United Kingdom
fireal.co.uk
+44 117 329 0090

Food by Sophie
1-15 Wine St,
 Bristol BS1 2BB, United Kingdom

Jamaica Street Stores
37-39 Jamaica St,
Bristol BS2 8JP, United Kingdom
+44 117 924 9294

Jerk King

UNIT 24 Ashley Down Rd,
Bishopston,
Bristol BS7 9JN, United
+44 7827 192522

Just Right LTE
St. Anne's, 8b Wootton Rd,
Brislington,
Bristol BS4 4AL, United Kingdom
+44 117 401 5969

Mama Cleo's Kitchen
388 Stapleton Rd, Easton,
Bristol BS5 6NQ, United
Kingdom

Mama P's
611 Fishponds Rd,
Bristol BS16 3AA, United
Kingdom
Mamma-ps.co.uk
+44 117 239 6718

Nadine's Caribbean Cafe
5 Stapleton Rd, Easton,
Bristol BS5 0QR, United
Kingdom

One Caribbean Restaurant
282 Lodge Causeway,
Bristol BS16 3RD, United
Kingdom
+44 117 958 6900

Real Habesha
146 Stapleton Rd, Easton,
Bristol BS5 0PU, United
Kingdom

Rice and Things
120 Cheltenham Rd, Cotham,

Bristol BS6 5RW, United
Kingdom
+44 117 924 4832

Roger Moore Caribbean Cuisine
329 Southmead Rd, Southmead,
Bristol BS10 5LW, United
Kingdom
rogermoorescarribbean.co.uk
+44 117 959 2278

St.Mary's Kitchen
212 Cheltenham Rd, St
Andrew's,
Bristol BS6 5QU, United
Kingdom
+44 117 924 1684

Star and Garter
33 Brook Rd, Montpelier,
Bristol BS6 5LR, United
Kingdom
+44 117 904 0509

The Caribbean Shack
312 Gloucester Rd, Horfield,
Bristol BS7 8TJ, United Kingdom
thecaribbeanshack.co.uk
+44 117 330 1863

The Kings Head
Kings Head, 277-279 Whitehall
Rd,
Whitehall, Bristol BS5 7BH,
United Kingdom
Thekingsheadsbristol.co.uk
+44 117 902 5452

Turtle Bay
Turtle Bay, 8 Broad Quay,

Bristol BS1 4DA, United Kingdom
+44 117 929 0209

Vybz
379 Filton Ave,
Bristol BS7 0LH, United Kingdom
+44 117 401 0061

Yummy Jaimaican Cuisine
90C High St,
Bristol BS16 5HL, United Kingdom
+44 7586 457672

Salons/Barbershops
CoCocheno
17 Nelson Street, Bristol, BS1 2LA
cococheno.co.uk
+44 117 925 7700

Tours
Walking Tour -Bristol slavery trail- It's self guided and more of the perspective of the slave owners and the 3 million Africans that came through this port.

*Visit Rosa Parks Lane

LIVERPOOL

Museum

International Slavery Museum
Liverpool L3 4AQ, United Kingdom

Restaurants

Absolute Jerk Liverpool
3-4, Parrs Corner, Liverpool, Bootle L20 5AJ, United Kingdom
+44 151 345 6636

Bala B's Soul Food Kitchen
Lodge Ln, Liverpool L8 0QW, United Kingdom
+44 151 345 1713

Bistro Noir
14 - 16 Lark Ln, Liverpool L17 8US,
United Kingdom
+44 151 728 9826

Coffee and Fandisha
5 Brick St, Liverpool L1 0BL,
United Kingdom
+44 151 708 6492

Coffee Lodge
57 Lodge Ln, Liverpool L8 0QE,
United Kingdom
+44 151 280 4652

Dee Delicious
67 Trispen Road
Liverpool
Merseyside
L11 6NE

Eat up Gud
Granby Street Market
+44 74 1359 2836

Ital Fresh
61 Jordan St, Liverpool
L1 0BP, United Kingdom :
+44 7720 925366

Mo'Bay Shack
Rum Punch Distributor
https://mobayshack.store/

Raggas
58 Smithdown Rd, Toxteth,
Liverpool L7 4JG, United
Kingdom
http://www.raggas.co.uk/
+44 15 1281 3241

Soul Cafe
114 Bold St, Liverpool
L1 4HY, United Kingdom
+44 151 708 9470

Treaty Pie
Business Park, Prescot Rd,
Old Swan, Liverpool L13 3AS,
United Kingdom
+44 7548 274560

Yamm Tree
yammtree@gmail.com
+44 7731 708103

Sweets/ Bakery

Desserts by Dre
http://www.dessertsbydre.co.uk/
info@dessertsbydre.co.uk

The Cheesecake Club
@the_cheesecake_club

LONDON

Brixton is the most well known black neighborhood but there are other areas with a large black population like South London and East London.

Notting Hill Carnival- September

Banks

FBN Bank (UK)
28 Finsbury Circus,
London,
EC2M 7DT
+44 20 7920 4920

Ghana International Bank
(GHIB)
67 Cheapside 1st Floor
City of London, EC2V 6AZ
+44 84 5605 6004

Guaranty Trust Bank (UK)
Limited
60-62 Margaret Street,
London W1W 8TF
+44 20 7947 9700

UBA Capital Europe Limited
https://www.ubagroup.com/

Union Bank (UK)Plc
1 King's Arms Yard London
EC2R 7AF.
+44 20 7920 6100

Zenith Bank (UK) Ltd
39 Cornhill
London
EC3V 3ND
United Kingdom
Tel: +44 (0)20 7105 3950
info@zenith-bank.co.uk

Beauty/ Cosmetics

Banks Pro Beauty
bankyprobeauty@yahoo.com
+44 7932823142

Damiva Beauty
damivabeauty@gmail.com
+44 74 3272 0588

Divaz Beauty London
Divazbeauty.co.uk
+44 75 3526 8964

Fatti Makeover
fattimcaulay@yahoo.co.uk
+44 78 4645 8420

Gorgeous Looks Makeover
alaoaminat2006@yahoo.co.uk
+44 7415417977

Gos Beauty Makeover
graceokunsanya@yahoo.co.uk
+44 79 0816 2050

Joy Adenuga
joyadenuga.com

Lizzie A 1
e_awosanya@hotmail.com
+44 79 4386 3792

Majado Beauty
majado.beauty@gmail.com

Ots Beauty
rasheeda@otsbeauty.co.uk
+44 79 3100 4232

Raffinee By Lola

www.raffineebylola.co.uk
+44 78 3003 0393
info@raffineebylola.co.uk

Ray Jeweled
info@rayjeweledbeauty.com
+44 77 1534 0481

Remsco Beauty
remcocreations.com
+44 79 0821 6206

Tee and bee makeover
tbee_011@yahoo.co.uk
+44 78 6871 9662

The Makeover Chic
demakeoverchic@gmail.com
+44 74 0100 5110

Tofar beauty makeup
arinefizyadunmo@yahoo.co.uk
+44 75 3434 9034

Touched by Rachel
info@touchedbyracheal.com
+44 74 1541 7977

True Glam Beauty
+44 74 9424 5243

Virtuous Beauty
Virtuoushairbeauty@gmail.com
+44 79 7652 5825

Yalliz Beauty
yewande_alli@yahoo.com
+44 78 2871 9135

Bookstore

Books of Africa
Booksofafrica.com
+44 20 8693 6426

New Beacon Books
 76 Stroud Green Road N4 3EN
London, UK
https://www.newbeaconbooks.co
m/

No Ordinary Book Shop
@noordinarybookshop

Pepukayi Books
366a High Road
Tottenham
London N17 9HT

Round Table Books
97 Granville Arcade,
Coldharbour Lane
Brixton, London
SW9 8PS

Brunch

Hip Hop Brunch London
https://www.hiphopbrunchldn.co
m/

Raggae Brunch
http://www.reggaebrunch.co.uk/l
ondon/

Entertainment

Kingdom Choir
https://kingdomchoir.com/

Fitness

Ball London- Basketball
community and pick up games
@ballislondon

Noire Fit Fest - Fitness Festival
for black athletes
https://noirefitfest.com/

Sports 100-App to find football
teams and games
Available in the app store

The Athletes Method-Personal
Training and Group Fitness
Sessions
http://www.theathletemethod.co
m/

Wedntplay-Fitness community
with Yoga, Pilates and other
fitness activities
https://www.wedntplay.com/

Museums

Black Cultural Archives
1 Windrush Square, Brixton
London SW2 1EF
info@bcaheritage.org.uk
+44 20 3757 8500

London Sugar and Slavery
Gallery

The Africa Centre
Arch 28, Old Union Yard Arches,
229 Union Street, London, SE1
0LR
+44 (0) 208 004 6436
info@africacentre.org.uk
Restaurants

805 Restaurant,
805 Old Kent Road,
Peckham, London SE15 1NX
+44 20 7639 0808
805restaurants.com

1251
107 Upper Street, Islington,
London N1 1QN
+44 7934 202269
1251.co.uk

Andi's Wadadli Kitchen at The
Crooked Billet
The Crooked Billet,84 Upper
Clapton Rd
E5 9JP London, UK
http://wadadlikitchen.com/
+44 7931 228613

Appestat
102 Islington High Street N1
8EG London, UK
+44 20 7226 5457
http://www.appestat.co.uk/

Aso Rock express
10 Bradbury Street, Dalston,
London N16 8JN
+44 207 923 7068
https://www.asorockfood.com

Ayannas
2 Yabsley Street, Poplar,
London E14 9RG
+44 20 3772 4140
Ayannaslondon.com

Balageru Restaurant
22 Blackstock Road

London N4 2DW

Banaadiri
342 Uxbridge Rd, Shepherd's
Bush,
London W12 7LL, United
Kingdom
+44 20 8740 8888

Belly's Taste of Jamaica
291 Hoxton Street
Shoreditch London
N15JX
+44 207 613 2111

Beza
8A Sayer Street, Elephant and
Castle,
London SE17 1FH
Bezaveganfood.com

Big Town
302 Walworth Road, Walworth
London SE17 2TE
http://www.bigtownrestaurants.c
om/
+44 20 7358 4327

Bokit'la
Montgomery Hall, 58 Kennington
Oval London,
London, SE115SW
+44 78 8986 4375

Brothers Cafe & Restaurant
552 High Rd, Tottenham,
London N17 9SY, United
Kingdom
+44 20 3556 7258

Brown Eagle - 4 locations

browneagle.co.uk
741 High Road Tottenham,
London N17 8AG

107 Old Church Road
Chingford London E4 6ST

586 Hertford Road
Enfield . EN3 5SX

234 High Road Wood Green,
London . N22 8HH

Cafe Caribbean
Pavilion Building, Old Spitalfields
Market, London E1 6EW
Spitalfields: +44 2073776443
https://cafe-caribbean.co.uk/

Calabash Bistro
12 Chapel Rd, Ilford IG1 2AG,
United Kingdom
http://www.calabashcuisine.co.u
k/
+44 20 8503 1664

Cally Muchie- 4 stall locations

THE KERB
Kings Cross
West India Quay
The Gherkin
Caribe
Unit S36 POP Brixton, 49 Brixton
Station Road, SW9 8PQ
https://www.caribeuk.com/
+44 75 1510 2724

Caribbean Spice
47 W Green Rd, Tottenham,

London N15 5BY, United
Kingdom
+44 20 8802 5000

Chicken kitchen
120 Goldhawk Rd, Shepherd's
Bush,
London W12 8HD, United
Kingdom
http://www.chickenkitchenuk.co
m/
+44 20 8735 0572

Chukus
274 High Road, Tottenham, N15
4aj
https://www.chukuslondon.co.uk/

Crepes and Cones
24 South End Cr01dn Croydon,
UK
+44 20 3730 6204
https://crepesandcones.com/

Deluxe Manna
135-137 High Cross Road,
tottenham
London N17 9NU, United
Kingdom
+44 208 801 8888

Eko Restaurant
160 Homerton High Road
Hackney
London E9 6JA
http://www.ekorestaurant.net/

Eat of Eden - 4 locations

Continents/Countries
https://eatofeden.co.uk/

Brixton Branch
4 Brixton Village, Coldharbour Lane
SW9 8PR
+44 20 7737 7566

Clapham Branch
6 Ascot Parade, Clapham Park Road
SW4 7EY
+44 20 7498 4412

Lewisham Branch
1 Goldcrest House, 32-64 Lee High Road
SE13 5FH
+44 20 8318 3139

Sheperd's Bush Branch
76 Shepherds Bush Road
W6 7PH
(020) 7348 0243

Enish - 5 locations
https://www.enish.co.uk/

Brixton
330a Coldharbour Lane
Brixton , London

Croydon
62 South End
Croydon CR0 1DP

Drums and Flats,
Boxpark, 18 Olympic Way,
Wembley Park, Wembley HA9 0JT
Drumsandflats.co.uk

Emba Soira
10 Crouch Hill, Stroud Green,
London N4 4AU, United Kingdom

Etta's Seafood Kitchen
85/86 Brixton Village
London SW9 8PS
+44 203 489 9394

Finchley Rd
299 Finchley Road
West Hampstead NW3 6DT

Fish Wings and Tings- 2 locations
https://www.fishwingsandtings.com/

Brixton Village
3 Granville Arcade, Coldharbour Lane,
Brixton, SW9 8PR

Caribbean Kitchen
67 Mare St, Hackney,
London E8 4RG, UK
+44 203 730 9952

Croydon (Box Park)
99 George St,
Croydon, CR0 1LD

Grannys Caribbean Takeaway
16 Stroud Green Road, London
London, N4 3SG
+44 20 7281 6974

Hacha Bar
378 Kingsland Road

London E8 4AA
https://www.hachabar.com/

Hanson Grill
224B Preston Rd,
Wembley HA9 8PB
+44 20 8904 4111

Healthy Eaters
17 Electric Avenue
London SW9 8JP
020 7274 4521
http://www.healthyeaters.co.uk/

Hilltop Roti
46-48 Drayton Green Rd,
West Ealing, W13 8RY
07961 869902

Homemade by Haddasah
@homemadebyhadassah
Instagram orders and delivery

Igochop
46 Camberwell Church Street
London
SE5 8QZ
+44 020 3581 4496
http://www.igochop.com/

Ikoyi
1 St James's Market,
St James's, London SW1Y 4AH
+44 20 3583 4660
ikoyilondon.com

Ilford
291-293 High Road
Ilford IG1 1NR

Island Buka

Flat 2, 160 162 Deptford High
Street,
London, Se8 3Pq
+44 20 8692 8397

Issa Vibe
181 Rye Lane, London,
SE154TP
+44 20 7732 8322
info@issaviberestaurant.co.uk

Jades Jerk
127 New Cross Rd, London
SE14 5DJ, United Kingdom
+44 20 3602 6873

Jamaica Patty Co.
26 new row, Covenant Garden,
London
http://www.jamaicapatty.co.uk/
+44 20 7836 3334
Jamaicapattyco@gmail.com

Jay Dees Caribbean Catering
28 Lancaster Road, London
W11 1QP
+44 20 7243 5969

JB's Soulfood
27A Peckham High Street
SE15 5EB London, UK

Jerk Munchies
Harringey
N15 4QT
https://www.jerkmunchies.co.uk/

Jerk Off BBQ
3 Creekside, Deptford, London
SE8 4SA,
United Kingdom

Jerkoffbbq.com

Jollof box
64 Kingsland High Street
Dalston Kingsland,
London E8 2LX England
Jollofbox.co.uk
+44 20 3488 1961

Jollof and Jerk
179A London Road.
Mitcham CR4 2JB
http://jollofnjerklondon.co.uk/

Kaffa Coffee- 2 locations
http://www.kaffacoffee.co.uk/

1 Gillett Street
Dalston London
N16 8AZ

6 Bradbury Street
Dalston\ London
N16 8JN

Kaieteur Kitchen
335-336 Elephant and Castle,
London SE1 6TB, United
Kingdom
+44 7466 616137

Kate's Cafe and Restaurant
174 Balaam St, London
E13 8RD, United Kingdom
+44 20 8586 6793

Kings Kitchen
Unity Y10, Action Business
centre , School Rd.
London, United Kingdom, NW10
6TD

http://home.kings.kitchen/

Kokobella Kitchen
Flat 15 Valley Heights 275
Godstone Road,
Croydon, CR3 0BD

Lekki Restaurant and Bar
323 Kingsland Rd, Dalston,
London E8 4DL, United Kingdom
+44 20 7923 2050

Leilani
14 Lavender Hill, Battersea,
London SW11 5RW
+44 20 7801 9322

Lewisham High St.
228 Lewisham High St,
London, SE13 6JU

Little Baobab
Littlebaobab.co.uk

Little Black Kitchen
107 Dunton Road
Old Kent Road
London, SE1 5HG
+44 7850 167350
https://little-black-
kitchen.business.site/

Lobster and Grill
12 High Street SM1 1HN
Sutton, UK
https://lobsterandgrill.co.uk/
+44 20 8722 0180

Lolak Afrique
38 Choumert Rd, Peckham,

London SE15 4SE, United
Kingdom
+44 20 7277 8912

Lulu's Kitchen
84 Stroud Green Road,
Haringey, N4 3EN
http://www.lulusrestaurant.co.uk/
haringey/

Mama Africa
25-27 Watford Way, London,
NW
NW4 3JH, United Kingdom
Mamaafricarestaurant.com

Mamacalabar
38 Vivian Avenue, Hendon
Central, London,
NW4 3XP United Kingdom
https://mamacalabar.co.uk/
+44 0 208 202 4660

Mamas Jerk
Arch 10
Deptford Market Yard
London
SE8 4NS
https://mamasjerk.com/

Negril
132 Brixton Hill,
Brixton, London SW2 1RS,
United Kingdom
+44 20 8674 8798
Negrilrestaurant.co.uk

Nigerian Food xpress
1 Faircross Parade, Longbridge
road,
Barking , United Kingdom

+44 20 8594 2805

Nickaysia
91 Dudden Hill Lane,
London, NW101BD
https://nickaycias.co.uk/

Ochi
226 Uxbridge RD,
Sheperds Bush, W12 7JD
https://ochitakeawayandcatering.
co.uk/

Only Jerkin
https://www.onlyjerkin.com/
+44 7709 844443

One Love Kitchen- 3 locations
https://www.onelove-
kitchen.co.uk/

Crouch Hill
9 Crouch Hill, London N4 4AP

Fenchurch
8 Fenchurch Place, London
EC3M 4PB

Maltby Street
41 Maltby Street, London SE1
3PA

One Stop
17-19 High Street, Harlesden,
London, NW10 4NE
+44 20 8961 6151

Pandaberry
2 Nether St, North Finchley,
London N12 0EL, United
Kingdom

+442034415089

Pepper & Spice
40 Balls Pond Rd, Dalston,
London N1 4AU, United
Kingdom
+44 20 7275 9818

Presidential Suya
162-164 Old Kent Road
London,
United Kingdom
020 7708 4491
PresidentialSuyaRestaurant@g
mail.com

Rayaan Restaurant
610 High Rd. Tottenham Hale,
london N17 9TA
+44 20 8001 2502
https://rayaanrestaurant.co.uk/in
dex.html

Red Rooster
45 Curtain Road,
Hackney, London EC2A 3PT
+44 20 3146 4545
Redroosterldn.com

Renee's Kitchen
reneesplantpowereddkitchen@g
mail.com
https://www.reneeskitchen.co.uk/

Rhythm Kitchen
257 Hoe Street,
Walthamstow, London E17 9PT
+44 20 8520 6112
Rhythmkitchen.co
Rock Steady Rum Lounge,
128 Gipsy Hill, Dulwich,

London SE19 1PL
+44 20 8670 4030
Rocksteadyrumlounge.com

Roti Kitchen
6 Leeland Road, West Ealing,
London W13 9HH
https://rotikitchen.com/

Roti Stop Ltd
36B Stamford Hill, Cazenove,
London N16 6XZ, United
Kingdom
+442088154433

Shelly Belly's
12b Palmerston Road E17 7
London, UK
http://www.shellybellys.com/

Somali Town
10 Gleneagle Rd, Streatham,
London SW16 6AB, United
Kingdom
+44 20 8835 8406

Something Ghanaian
217 Kingsbury Road
London, NW99PQ

So Nice , One Stop
Unit 1, 2-4 Upper Tollington
Park, Stroud Green,
London N4 3EL, United Kingdom

Spices Jamaican Cuisine
371-373 High Road
London NW10 2JR
http://spicesjamaican.co.uk/
+44 2034 172431

Spinach and Agushi - 3 locations
https://www.spinachandagushi.com/

6 Exmouth Market,
Farringdon, London

70 Broadway Market,
London EQ 4QJ

174 Portobello Rd, Notting Hill,
London W11 2EB

Stoney Hill
59 Leytonstone Rd,
London E15 1JA,
United Kingdom
+44 20 3583 2246

Stork
13-14 Cork Street, Mayfair
London W1S 3NS
+44 20 3973 9307
Storkrestaurant.com

Sweet Handz
217 Holloway Road,
London, N7 8DL

Swift Caribbean Delights
27 Homerton High St, Clapton,
London E9 6JP, United Kingdom
+44 208 533 6060

Survivor - 2 Locations

6 Sandringham Rd, Dalston,
London E8 2LP, United Kingdom
+44 20 3774 5314

98 Arlington Rd,
London NW1 7HT, United
Kingdom
+44 20 7383 0788
Talking Drum London
610 O.K.R. London SE15 1 JB
https://www.talkingdrum.co.uk/
+44 20 7732 8377

Tasty African Restaurant
83 Longbridge Rd,
Barking IG11 8TG, United
Kingdom
+44 20 8594 5808

Tasty Jerk
88 Whitehorse Ln, South
Norwood,
London SE25 6RQ, United
Kingdom
+44 20 8653 3222

The Taste Box
4A Gillespie Road
London, N5 1LN

The Real Jerk
89 Streatham Hill
London, England
SW2 4UD
http://www.therealjerk.co.uk/

The West Indian Bake Company,
Mercato Metropolitano, 42
Newington Causeway,
Elephant and Castle, London
SE1 6DR
Westindianbake.co
+44 20 8671 1171

Three Little Birds,

412 Coldharbour Lane, Brixton
London SW9 8LF
Threelittlebirdsja.com

Too Sweet
63 Chatsworth Rd, Lower
Clapton,
London E5 0LH, United Kingdom
+44 20 8525 8168

Tracks and Records,
94 Middlesex Street, Spitalfields
London E1 7EZ
Tracksandrecords.uk

Trailer Happiness
177 Portobello Road,
Notting Hill W11 2DY
http://trailerh.com/

Trap Kitchen
76 Bedford Hill
London, United Kingdom
Trapkitchen.co.uk
+44 7568 521694

Tribe
22 Streatham High Rd,
Streatham Hill, London SW16
1DB
+447341937812
Tribev.co

Trinidad Roti Shop
27 Craven Park Road NW10
London, UK
http://www.trinidadrotishop.co.uk
/
+44 20 8838 4800

Tummy Comfort
8 Princes Parade
Golders Green Road
London NW11 9PS UK
+44 20 8455 6498

Uncle John's
76 W Green Rd
Tottenham, London
N15 5NS UK
https://theunclejohnsbakery.com/

Umana Yana
294 Croxted Road
Herne Hill, London, SE24 9DA
http://umanayana.co.uk/
+44 20 8671 8227

Wha Gwan
179 Garratt Lane, Wandsworth,
London, SW184DP

What's On The Menu Ish
@whatsonthemenuish
Truman Market - Saturday
Walthamstow - Sunday

Wolkite
82 Hornsey Rd,
London N7 7NN
+44 207 700 6427
http://www.wolkiterestaurant.com
/

Young Vegans Pizza Shop
393 Cambridge Heath Road
London E2 9RA
+44 (0)7494 333639
Youngveganspizzashop.com

Zeret Kitchen

216-218 Camberwell Road. SE5
0ED
+44 20 7701 8587
http://zeretkitchen.co.uk/

Zoe's Ghana Kitchen
56 Dace Rd.
E32NQ, London England

Salons/Barbershops

3thirty
330 Old St London
EC1V 9DR
www.3thirty.co.uk

Adornment 365
81 Acre Lane, Brixton, London,
SW2 5TN
Adornment365.com

Afrotherapy
235 Fore St London
N18 2TZ

Chop Chop
362 Old St, London EC1V 9LT
chopchoplondon.com

C suite Hair and beauty
190 Trafalgar Road, London
SE10 9TZ
C-suitelounge.com
+44 0208 858 8026

Darth Fader
600 Longbridge Road
Dagenham London
RM8 2AJ

Elite

Sidney Store, Sidney Rd
London SW9 0TS
www.elitehairlounge.co.uk

F4FADE
12 Leeland Road
London W13 9HH
www.f4fade.co.uk

Hair Force one!
134 Cranbrook Road
London IG1 4LZ
www.hairforce-1.co.uk

Hair Lounge
347 Portobello Rd, London W10
5SA
Charlottemensah.com

5ive Hype Coiffure Battersea
186 Lavender Hill
London SW11 5TQ
www.hypecoiffure.com

Junior Green
55 Kensington Church St,
Kensington, London W8 4BA
Juniorgreen.com
+44 0207 752 0620

Mimi et Mina
16 Needham Road W11 2RP
London, UK
https://www.mimietmina.com/

Morris Code
357 Archway Rd
London N6 4EJ
www.morrisroots.com

My Hair Bar
22 Warren St
London W1T 5LU
www.myhairbar.com

Radiant London
178 Jamaica Road,
Bermondsey,
London, SE16 4RT
Radiantlondon.com
+44 2072318833

RXB Barbers
80 Brixton Road
London SW9 6BH

Slider Cuts
176 SliderCuts Studios
Hackney Road
London E2 7QL
www.alidercuts.com

Starboy Barber
256 Kilburn High Road
London NW6 2BY
Ziuzo
84 Lee High Rd
London SE13 5PT
www.ziuzo.com

Sweets/Bakery

Aries Bakehouse
99 Acrelane, Brixton
London, England SW25TU, GB
https://aries-bakehouse.square.site/
02080012970
Ariesbakehouse@yahoo.com

Dalhousie
1 WESTOW STREET
CRYSTAL PALACE, SE19
http://www.dalhousie.london/
+44 20 8771 5770

Dark Sugars Chocolates
141 Brick Lane
London, E1 6SB
www.darksugars.co.uk

Dark Sugars Cocoa House
124-126 Bricks Lane
London E1 6RU

Midnight Munchies
332b Camberwell New Road
Camberwell
SE5 0RW
United Kingdom
+44 20 7733 1237

Saint Aymes
59 Connaught St, St George's Fields,
London W2 2BB, United Kingdom
Saintaymes.com

Tastopia
Town Hall Approach Rd.
Tottenham Green London,
United Kingdom London, UK
+44 7534 504800

The Treats club
https://thetreatsclub.com/

Tours

Black History Walks

www.blackhistorywalks.co.uk

Travel

Travel. Eat. Slay
http://traveleatslay.com/
info@traveleatslay.com

Wind Collective
https://thewindcollective.com/

Black British Travel Meetup
info.bbtmu@gmail.com

Wellness

Pempamsie - 4 locations
https://www.pempamsie.com/

102 BRIXTON HILL,
LONDON SW2 1AH

219 LONDON ROAD,
LONDON CR4 2JD

1 Goldcost House
32-64 Lee High Road
Lewisham London SE13 5FH

375B Hoe St. Walthamstow
London E17 9AP

Manchester

Beauty/ Cosmetics

Chandelles Browns and Beauty
7 Moss lane, Whitefield, Bury,
United Kingdom
@Chandelles_browsnbeauty
Chandelle4@hotmail.com

Fitness

J7 Health Centre
Unit 6, 73 Old Market St,
Manchester. M9 8DX
WWW.J7HEALTHCENTRE.CO.
UK

Restaurants

Bubz Kitchen
+44 161 226 4104

Foul Mouths food
https://www.fowlmouths.co.uk/

Island Vibe Bar and Restaurant
414-416 Wilbraham Rd,
Chorlton-cum-Hardy,
Manchester M21 0SD, United
Kingdom
http://islandvibebarandrestaurant
.com/

Jerk Junction
170 Manchester Rd Manchester
M16 0DZ United Kingdom

Little Rock english and
caribbean cuisine
241 princess road M16 7
Manchester, UK
+44 161 226 4104

Pull Up Bar
14-16 Swan St, Manchester
M4 5JN, United Kingdom
+44 161 637 9370

Trap Kitchen
6-8 Hillkirk St,

Manchester M11 3EZ,
United Kingdom

Salons/Barbershop

Glam Gorgeous
290 Barlow Rd, Manchester M19
3JB
glamgorgeoushairandbeauty.co
m
+44 0161 667 1544

Self Identity
WWW.SELFIDENTITY.CO.UK

Simply Faded Barbershop
146 Butterstile Ln, Prestwich,
Manchester M25 9TJ, United
Kingdom
+44 7729 543118

Sweets/Bakery

Minikin Bake Box
minikinbakebox@gmail.com

Wellness

Healing Hands
healinghands67@yahoo.com

NEW CASTLE

The significance of New Castle is
large as it was a place African
Americans fled to in England
during slavery to recieve
freedom. Frederick perhaps the
most famous leader of the 19th
century is one who received his
freedom here due tot heir anti
slavery views.. It was a safe
haven for many and the Tyne
Concert hall was instrumental for
black people during the 19th
century. Martin Luther King Jr.
Also visited here and gave a
commencement speech at one of
the University's.

Grocery

Kenechi afro/ Caribbean store
258 Clara St, Benwell,
Newcastle upon Tyne
NE4 8PY, United Kingdom
+44 191 273 5422

Osas Afro Caribbean Food Shop
438 Westgate Rd, Newcastle
upon Tyne
NE4 9BN, United Kingdom

Restaurants

Deagape Kitchen
unit 6, Restoration House,
Norham Rd, Newcastle upon
Tyne,
North Shields NE29 7TN, United
Kingdom
House of Jollof
94 - 102 Blandford St, Newcastle
upon Tyne
NE1 3BT, United Kingdom

Meal Castle
1A Mill Ln, Newcastle upon Tyne
NE4 6QB, United Kingdom

Mosob
24 Scotswood Rd, Newcastle
upon Tyne
NE4 7JB, United Kingdom

Mosobgezana.co.uk
+44 191 903 2139

Soul Foods Catering
247 Philip St, Newcastle upon
Tyne
NE4 5BH, United Kingdom
+44 191 340 9294

Tony's Kitchen
377 Elswick Rd, Benwell,
Newcastle upon Tyne NE4 8DY,
United
+44 191 273 5666

Salons/Barbershops

Aurel Afro Caribbean
Hairdresser
Liddle Rd, Newcastle upon Tyne
 NE4 5JE, United Kingdom

Glo Afro Caribbean Hair Shop
Bavington Dr, 17, Newcastle
upon Tyne
NE5 2HS, United Kingdom

Hair by Ruth Codinha
6, Central Station, Forth St,
Newcastle upon Tyne
NE1 3NZ, United Kingdom
+44 191 261 2211

Hair City
55 Clayton St, Newcastle upon
Tyne
NE1 5PW, United Kingdom

Lux Styles
42A Elswick Rd, Newcastle upon
Tyne

NE4 6JE, United Kingdom
Ruth Codinha
6 Central Station, Forth St,
Newcastle upon Tyne NE1 3NZ
Hairbyruthcodinha.co.uk
+44 1912612211

IRELAND

Black and Irish- Facebook
community

https://irishblackowned.com/ -
Black business listings

Belfast

Irawo
+353 83 404 4334
https://getsoupbucket.com/
irawo.experience@gmail.com

Cork

Restaurants

Tee Pot
dehinbo.t@gmail.com
+353 83 079 5318
@tee_potty

Salons/Barbershops

The Lace HQ
https://thelacehq.com/
@thelacehq

Sweets/Bakery

Celebrate With Cake
corkcelebrate@gmail.com
+353 85 778 9088

Drogheda

Laid by Emmy
laidbyemmy@outlook.com
@laidbyemmy

Dublin

Beauty/Cosmetics

Alliyah's Nails
@alliyah.nails

Ara Nailed It
Ara.nailedit

Arlys Cosmetics
http://www.arlycosmetics.com/

Lizzys Nails
@lizzysnails_

Grocery

Mamashee
Merrion Square S, Saint Peter's,
Dublin 2, Ireland
https://mamashee.com/
@mamashee
+353 85 167 4563

Marhaba Stores
2 Lower Eyre, Street ,
Newbridge, Kildare, Ireland
marhabastorenewbridge@gmail.
com
+353 86 894 1960

@marhaba_stores

Restaurants

Afro Chow
http://afchow.com/

Cuisine Wise
Cuisine_wise
+353 83 186 2795
mariaolajide56@gmail.com

Gursha
394 N circular Rd, Dublin 7
@Gursha_Ie

Hadolf T Cuisine
Unit 3 kylemore south park
Ballyfermot
hadolftcuisine@gmail.com
+353 86 328 4381

Heritage
+353 89 953 6095
@heritage.dublin

Lamis Kitchen Ireland
www.lamiskitchen.com
+353 089 977 7838

Lil Portie Caribbean Kitchen
250 square Coffee, Williams
park Rathmines, Ireland D06
KX90
Lilportie.com

Lone Catering
Lonecatering.com
+353 89 956 4273
@lonecatering

Meras Kitchen
+353 89 950 8695
mercyadelabu@gmail.com

Mimis Kitchen
mimiskitchenwings.typeform.com

Pretty Faces Dishes
@prettyfacesdishes
+353 87 361 4267

Ruby Tuesday's Soul Food
14-15 Dame Lane, Dublin 2, D02
XC91
+353 85 100 9426
www.rubytuesdays.ie
rubytuesdaysoulfood@gmail.co
m

Surulere
info@surulere.ie
+353 87 387 8760

The Vegan Honey Pot
theveganhoneypot@gmail.com
+353 86 419 5653

Salons/Barbershops

Anne Brigitte Tcheudji
@dijonaise_hair_and_beauty

Bangu Afro Salon Dublin
unit 3 kylemore park north
Dublin, Ireland Dublin 10
@bangu.ie

Banks Parlour
https://banksparlour.com/

Crochet Queen Creations

cqcstyling@gmail.com

Designer Cutzz
Unit GB1 Sitecast Industrial
Estate, Greenhills Road, Tallaght
D24, Dublin Ireland
https://www.designercuts.ie/

Elegance bridal Touch
@elegance_bridal_touch

HBA Studio
unit 7 westpark gate courthouse
square, dublin, tallaght, d24

Hair by Glo Glo
@hairb.bygloglo

I am Beauty Dublin
@Iambeautydublin

LA Beauty Dublin
labeautydublin@gmail.com
+353 85 835 2614

Lombe Barbers
@lombe_barbers
Unit6 Wespark Gate, Oldbawn
Road Tallaght, Ireland Dublin24
+353 85 106 0629

Miss Mercy Makeup Artistry
http://www.callmercy.com/
+353 87 776 0942

Poised By Suliat
@poisedbysuliat

The Studio by Marco Dias
13 Oxford Lane
@thestudioie

Tray Chic Designs
https://www.traychicdesigns.com/

YFA Hair
@yfahair_
infoyfahair@gmail.com

Sweets/ Bakery

Keva's Food & Rum Cake Co
kevasfoodco.net
info@kevasfoodco.com
+353 85 763 5239

Petite Gateaux
Petite_x_geteaux

Nectar & Ambrosia Cakes
nectarandambrosiacakes@gmail.com
+353 89 456 9992

Nourish Delight
nourishdelightirl@gmail.com
+353 87 364 7893

Nu's Cakes
info@nuscakes.com
https://www.nuscakesirl.com/

The Cookie Lounge
www.thecookielounge.ie/orde
Galway

Kingz Kitchen

Kildare
Beauty/Cosmetics

Make up by Mehe
@makeupbymehe

Leitrim
Accommodation

Quay Rest Bed and Breakfast
9 Shannon Quays, Rooskey, Co.
Leitrim, N41 PY77

Louth
Sweets/Bakery

Simmz Cuisine
@simmzcuisine

Moneygall
Historic Landmarks

Barack Obama plaza

Navan

Salons/Barbershop

Izzy The Barber
The Drive, 3, Navan
@Izzyjnrdabarber

Westport

Beauty/Cosmetics

Kennedy Beauty Studios
Kennedybeautystudios@gmail.com

+353 85 107 3462

SCOTLAND

Afrifest Scottland -
https://www.afrifestscotland.com/

Africa in Motion Film Festival -
October to november
https://www.africa-in-motion.org.uk/
@aimfilmfest

Rum Company/Distillery
https://www.matuggarum.com/

Community

Edinburgh Caribbean
Association
Aberdeeneshire

Farming

The artisan grower
AB52 6QH Aberdeen, UK

Restaurants

Bon Appelit Cuisine
@bonappelitcuisine_aberdeen

Eatablesfc
http://eatablesfc.com/

FHA Kitchen
27 Kettlehills Crescent,
Aberdeen, AB16 5TA
www.fhakitchen.com

Finger Dips

Auldearn Gardens AB12 5ND
Aberdeen, UK
http://www.fingerdips.co.uk/

Healthy African Flavours
www.keephealthyafricandiet.com

Jp soulfood
@jpsoulfood

Jollof Ninja
@jollofninja

My Kitchen -Catering
+44 7833 141232
adenikefamakinwa@gmail.com

Tasty T's Cuisine
563 George Street AB253
Aberdeen, UK

Sweets/Bakery

Dimbim Speciality Cakes
14 Morven Circle AB32 6WD
Aberdeen, UK

Perez Cakes
Scotsmill Crescent AB21 0JG
Blackburn, UK

O'Caykx
22 Schoolhill, Aberdeen City
Centre AB10 1JX Aberdeen, UK

Tino's Delightz
http://tinosdelightz.com/

Eidinburgh

Black history walks Eidinburgh-

@ caribscot
edincarib@gmail.com
07429 540849

Restaurants

Go Go Beets
165 Portobello High Street

Knights Kitchen
166 Leith Walk, Edinburgh
RiveRLife
84 Dalry Road, Edinburgh
info@riverlifeedinburgh.co.uk

Salons/ Barbershops

A touch of silk
131 gorgie road, Edinburgh ,
United Kingdom

Braiding World
287-291 Leith Walk, Edinburgh
EH6 8PD, United Kingdom

Christine African Hair , weave
and braids
5, 8 Hyvot Park, Edinburgh
EH17 8PR, United Kingdom

Culture Lounge
135 Great Jct St, Edinburgh EH6
5JB, United Kingdom

Estate Salon
267b Leith Walk, Edinburgh EH6
8PD, United Kingdom
estatesalon.co.uk

Floxee Hair salon

352 Gorgie Rd, Edinburgh EH11
2RQ, United Kingdom

Sweets/Bakery

Caked by Catherine
veecat5@hotmail.com

Glasglow

Grocery

Main Africa Store
486 Duke St, Glasgow G31 1QF,
United Kingdom

Zimba mama Africa Training
942 Govan Rd, Govan, Glasgow
G51 3AF, United Kingdom
+44 141 328 9880

Restaurant

Apo Kitchen
1391 Gallowgate, Parkhead,
Glasgow G31 4EX, United
Kingdom
apokitchen.co.uk

Bantaba Afro Caribbean
Restaurant
507 London Rd, Glasgow G40
1NQ, United Kingdom
Calabash African Restaurant
57 Union Street, Glasgow. G1
3RB.
01412212711

Comforter in the city
50 Dundas St, Glasgow G1 2AQ,
United Kingdom
+44 141 332 0031

Horn of Africa
672 Eglinton St, Glasgow G5
9RP, United Kingdom
+44 141 237 8332

Pepper Soup Joint
175 Allison St, Govanhill,
Glasgow G42 8RX, United
Kingdom
+44 141 423 5446

Rum Shack
657 - 659 Pollokshaws Rd,
Glasgow G41 2AB, United
Kingdom
+44 141 237 4432
rumshackglasgow.com

Taste of home African
Restaurant
136 Nelson street G5 8EJ
Glasgow, UK

Salons/Barbershop

Beauty Splendor
22 Oykel Crescent. Glasgow.
G33 1FD
info@beautysplendour.com
Tel: +44 7580632727

Degenesis Salon
150 gallowgate, Glasgow, United
Kingdom

Ema hair salon
207 Maryhill Road G20 7XJ
Glasgow, UK

Glasgow Braids and cornrows
ginaobande@yahoo.com

Glow and Shine Boutique
278 gallowgate, Glasgow, United
Kingdom

Snmhair Xtensions
15 Westmuir Street, Glasgow,
United Kingdom

WALES

National Windrush Day - June

Community organizations

Caribbean Heritage Cymru
Nigerians in Wales Association
North Wales Africa Society
South Wales Jamaican Society
Wrexham African Community

Cardiff

Restaurant

Irie shack
106–110 Woodville Road,
Cardiff, CF24 4EE

Rasta shack
Highbury place Cf54lp Cardiff,
UK

TheCaribbean Way
1-3 Dumballs Road CF105FG
Cardiff, UK

170

Continents/Countries

Salons/Barbershops

GLAM WEAVE Cardiff weaves &
braids in Cardiff
13 A
Broadway,roath,adamsdown
CF24 1NF Cardiff, UK

Luscious Queen Hair
8b broadway CF24 1NF Cardiff,
UK

Sheer Inspiration hair salon
87 Tudor Street,Riverside Cf11
6ad Cardiff, UK

Newport

Grocery
Afro Caribbean Food Store
12 Cardiff Rd, Newport NP20
2ED

Olumo Foods
59 Bondgate Darlington DL3 7JJ

Restaurants

 Dutchy's Jamaican Jerk Shack
15 North Street, Newport NP20
1JZ Wales
+44 1633 215048

Habesha Ethiopian
57 Commercial Road,
Newport, Gwent, NP20 2PF.

Irie Shack Bakery
396-398 Corporation Rd,
Newport NP19 0GA

Vees Island Twist
246 Corporation Rd, Newport
NP19 0DZ

Shaktis caribbean cuisine
122 Commercial St, Kingsway
Centre, Newport

Salons/Barbershops

Glossy Locks
 63 Commercial St NP20 1LQ
Newport, UK

V's Hair Salon
29 skinner street NP20 1HB
Newport, UK